More Praise for *Dreaming Lessons*

"Abby Bloom speaks to us as a personal coach would, sharing her story in ways that shine a light on our own possibilities. I highly recommend this book to you if you'd like a practical mentor to guide you, step-by-step, toward goals that may be more reachable than you ever imagined."

—Nancy Speer
Owner and principal, Cincinnatus

"*Dreaming Lessons* is a workshop in a book; a guide into a place of deep calm, awakening, confidence, and inspired realism. Abby Bloom coaches us to dream beyond the day to day; to pay attention to our life; and to step out boldly, claiming what is deeply clear and joyfully alive in us! *Dreaming Lessons* is a book for all of us because our dreams awaken us to new possibilities at every stage of life."

—The Rev. Dr. Lucy A. Forster-Smith
**Sedgwick Chaplain to the University,
Harvard University**

"Abby Bloom has shared her hard-earned wisdom and created a guide that coaches all of us in easy-to-understand steps so we can each start living our own dreams."

—Christine D'Amico
Coach, educator, and founder of OpenMinds

DREAMING LESSONS

Recognize and Reach for Your Dreams

Abby Bloom

Dreaming Lessons:
Recognize and Reach for Your Dreams

© 2015 by Abby Bloom. All rights reserved.

Published by East 26th Street Press, Minneapolis, Minnesota.

ISBN: 978-0-9864318-0-7

Cover art: © Voyagerix www.fotosearch.com
Cover and book design: Zan Ceeley, Trio Bookworks, triobookworks.com
Author photo: Tom Bloom
Illustrations on pages 61 and 69: Claudia Collver

Abby Bloom is available to speak to book clubs and other groups. To invite her to speak or to learn about her workshops, visit dreaminglessons.com.

Discounts for bulk purchases by nonprofits, schools, corporations, or other organizations may be available. Write to dreaminglessons@gmail.com to inquire.

Aside from brief passages in a published review, no part of this book may be reproduced or transmitted in any form or by any means, electronic or mechanical, including all technologies known or later developed, without written permission from the publisher.

For reprint permission, write to dreaminglessons@gmail.com.

For
Ava and Willa,
Alex and Ari

Contents

Preface
ix

Acknowledgments
xii

Lesson 1
Don't Believe Everything You Think
1

Lesson 2
You Deserve to Dream
9

Lesson 3
You Already Have What You Need
17

Lesson 4
Some Dreams Are Impossible—But They Are Clues
37

Lesson 5
Do Your Homework, Consider Trade-Offs, Then Decide
47

Lesson 6
Address Obstacles and Focus on Elements
63

Lesson 7
Start Without Knowing the End
73

Lesson 8
Relationships Pave the Way for Luck
83

Lesson 9
Our Natural State Is Calm
91

Lesson 10
One Good Thing Leads to Another
103

Closing Words:
Take Charge of Your Life
123

Additional Notes
125

Preface

For more than a dozen years now, my husband, Tom, and I have lived part of every year aboard our sailboat, first around the Mediterranean Sea, then in the Caribbean. During the winter months we live on board, island hopping as the spirit moves us, resting at anchor where we choose. We keep our boat shipshape—there's always something to fix, and we spend part of most days working—but otherwise, we enjoy a leisurely outdoor life. We eat our meals in the cockpit, swim from the boat, hike in the parks, take the bus to town, see the sights, shop in the markets, visit with friends. When spring comes, we return to the States, where we divide our time between our apartment in Minneapolis and our cabin on the south shore of Lake Superior. In the city we enjoy children, grandchildren, friends, and the delights of town. At the cabin, we attend to chores and projects and then kick back, walk the beach, putter. We are retired, though we work part-time in the fall.

Does this sound like a dream? It is. I'm living *my* dream life, and I'm writing to help *you* discover how to live yours. You don't need to be a person of wealth or privilege to realize your dreams. I'm not and never have been.

My parents were first-generation Americans, my grandparents all Russian Jewish émigrés. Everyone was poor. Mom and Dad married during the Depression and had three children. Economically, we remained lower middle class. Neither Mom nor Dad had gone to college, but they were cultured and ambitious for us. They pushed us to do well in school and were fussy about our behavior and language at home. They pinched pennies to take us to museums and theater. They played classical music and American standards on our record player, and they were readers. They strapped themselves financially to send me and my brother and sister to college.

Some of my parents' messages were life enhancing, and some were not. I am grateful that they shared with me their love of language and the arts; I embrace that love. I also absorbed two unhelpful, unspoken messages from them. One was that to do anything really wonderful, a person had to have more money than we had; the other was that life was a serious business—our family was not lighthearted. For years I let those messages prevent me from recognizing my dreams and working toward them. The obstacles you face might be different from mine, but perhaps they include a belief that you can't fulfill your most cherished wishes. I believe you can.

For many years I followed a conventional path, doing more or less what other people expected. I graduated from high school, completed a college degree, married. I then moved with my more adventurous husband to India, where he supervised a group of Peace Corps volunteers for two years. My parents were horrified by this move—my first experience with adventure. I lived in an Indian neighborhood, shopped in the bazaars, learned to speak Hindi, travelled. I met young Americans in India, my contemporaries, who were pursuing their dreams. While I wasn't yet able to recognize dreams of my own, I believe my experiences in India sowed the seeds for my finally—finally!—beginning to acknowledge my dreams and make them come true.

The year we returned to the States, 1969, our son, Ben, was born. I became a schoolteacher, later moving twice for my husband's career and adjusting my work around his. Over the eighteen years of our marriage, my husband's drinking gradually increased, and our lives grew harsher. He steadily refused to address his drinking, and in 1984, when I was forty-one, we divorced. By that time, he had managed to drink and gamble away much of what we had. With Ben in high school, I refocused on my career—I moved from working in the public sector to the private—and I began to create the experiences I describe in this book. In 2002, eighteen years after my divorce and well into making my dreams come true, I married Tom, and we began our sailing adventure.

So I didn't begin dreaming until middle age, and although that may seem late, I'm glad I didn't wait longer. If you are a young person reading this, it's not too early to start recognizing and following your dreams. If you are middle-aged or older, it's not too late.

My current life didn't happen *to* me. It's the culmination of almost thirty years of dreaming and choosing deliberately to make my dreams come true, one at a time. Whenever I realized a dream, friends would ask, "How did you manage to do that?"

At last I took their questions seriously and sorted through my thoughts, feelings, and experiences to see what it took to recognize and follow my path. I began writing *Dreaming Lessons* as a result. While I was writing it, I developed and offered a workshop, also called Dreaming Lessons, based on the themes I was discovering. I used the workshop to refine my thoughts and test the exercises in the book. By creating this book, I have a chance to realize another dream: helping *you* recognize and live *your* dreams.

Each of the chapters that follow begins with a story from my life in which I reached for a dream. I share what I learned from that experience and identify key themes and concepts. Many people have shared with me their stories about reaching for a dream, and you'll find some of those here as well. Then I offer questions and exercises to help you explore and reflect on the themes of the chapter and how they apply to you and your dreams. I encourage you to write down your thoughts directly in this book in the spaces provided. What you create here will ultimately serve as both a record of your journey and a reminder to keep reaching for your dreams.

The life Tom and I lead now is beyond our dreams. And while it suits us, it certainly wouldn't suit everyone. But whatever you dream of—climbing a mountain, cooking a gourmet dinner, starting a small business, visiting a place you've never been, making more time for yourself, or any other large or small dream—please accept this book as an invitation.

Truly, if I can make my dreams come true, so can you.

Acknowledgments

Thank you, Joe Bailey and Mavis Karn, for teaching me the principles. Thank you, Elizabeth Jarrett Andrew, for showing me that if the writer isn't learning, the work will not be interesting, and for your careful reading of my first and second drafts. Thank you, Christine Sikorski, for your help with later drafts and for applying the ideas in my book to your life. Thank you, members of my writing group, especially John Evans, Lucy Forster-Smith, and Debra Palmquist, for your reading, for your questions and suggestions, and for sticking with me. Thank you, Beth Wallace, for your focused feedback and enthusiastic encouragement. Thank you, Claudia Collver, for your visual clarity and for your drawings. Thank you, Beth Wright and colleagues at Trio Bookworks, for guidance, for your designing ways, and for spit and polish. Thank you, friends and family, for your stories. I could not have realized this dream without each of you.

And most of all, thank you, Tom, my sweet, comic valentine, for making my life a dream every day.

Don't Believe Everything You Think

What are you telling yourself that might not be true?
What habits of thinking are getting in your way?
Noticing is a dreaming skill.

One day in 1986, when I was in my early forties and living near Minneapolis, I was talking on the phone with my dad, who lived in Philadelphia. He was telling me about a major exhibit he had seen at the National Gallery of Art in Washington, DC. It was about to close, and he wanted me to see it. I longed to go, but the only other place the show would travel to was San Francisco. And there I was, a hard-working, home-owning, single mom, accustomed to keeping my nose to the grindstone and thinking smallish, and automatically I thought, *I can't go to San Francisco for an art show. Oh well.* And I noticed the familiar feeling of disappointment and resignation: something I longed for was for other people, not for me.

Then I started daydreaming about the exhibit Dad had described. It recreated eight shows held in Paris between 1874 and 1886 by the painters now known as Impressionists: Renoir's portraits and convivial gatherings, Degas's

dancers, Monet's gardens, the landscapes of Cézanne. I remembered the Impressionist shows Dad and I had seen over the years, beginning when I was very young, at home in Philadelphia, and in New York and Washington, DC. Once I was grown, I continued to attend museum exhibits of Impressionists and artists of other schools, sometimes with my dad when I was visiting my parents and often on my own. I felt enhanced, richer after seeing a fine exhibit, glad to have a connection with artists and art over the centuries. When I hadn't been to a museum for a while, I would begin yearning to make that connection again. But would I travel across the country to see an exhibit, even this one? I didn't think so.

And right then, uncharacteristically, surprisingly, I asked myself, *Why can't I go?* And then, more importantly, *What would it take for me to go? Well*, I answered, *I have a few vacation days I could take, and a couple of frequent flyer tickets from my new job.* (See Lesson 3: You Already Have What You Need.) And I told myself, *Other people travel from Minneapolis to San Francisco for a weekend. Maybe I can go.*

On an impulse, I called old friends who had moved to San Francisco, and they encouraged me to come. When they tried and failed to get tickets for the sold-out show, they said, "Come anyway. People often return tickets they can't use."

At the time, my son was sixteen, and he was surprised at my plan. "That doesn't sound like you, Mom," he said. But when Ben asked if he could go with me, I thought, *Why not?* And so we both went. My two frequent flyer tickets were for different airlines. Ben flew on Northwest, and I flew on the old Republic Airlines. After we landed, I remember Ben's saying, "We got on the planes and flew out here just like other people get on the bus." As if we did it all the time.

Our friends met us at the airport and took us to the de Young Museum in Golden Gate Park, where we had tickets within an hour. It was so easy. I wondered why I had hesitated and thought a trip like this was something I couldn't do.

At the museum, I lost myself in one magnificent painting after another, shaking my head, catching my breath, and feeling moved, sometimes to tears. As I walked slowly through each of the eight exhibits, I thought about how, during the late nineteenth century, the Académie Française, official determiner of French taste in art, shunned these painters and their work. In defiance, the painters held their own exhibits, the very ones duplicated here. How could these lively, colorful, evocative works have been so completely rejected? I wondered whether, like some of the French public at the time, I would have loved these paintings then.

After seeing the show, Ben and I spent the long weekend with our friends, enjoying their home, the mountains, and the beach, before flying back to Minneapolis.

Later I realized that *noticing* my disappointment and then *rethinking* my assumption that I couldn't go had been a breakthrough for me. For once, I hadn't automatically believed what I thought, and in noticing and questioning my thinking, I made my first dream come true. It was to be the first of many.

What I Learned: Just Because I Think Something Doesn't Mean It's True

I had long thought making dreams come true was for other people—people who were richer, smarter, more enterprising, *different* from me. I told myself that the folks who vacationed in Florida during spring break didn't feel obligated to visit family in a northern city, as I did. The couple who spent a museum-and-theater weekend in New York had no children. The guy who bought a thirty-foot boat and taught himself to sail was stronger than I was, more mechanically inclined, more confident. The woman who had a cabin on Lake Superior had more money. I focused on the differences I imagined between them and me, and on all the good, practical reasons not to attempt something unusual, extravagant.

And I never questioned those assumptions.

All that changed when, after automatically thinking, *Oh well, there's no way I could go*, I recognized a dream in my yearning to see the Impressionist show. I thought, *Wait a minute, why can't I?* and then asked myself, for the first time, *What would it take for me to do it?*

When I rejected my automatic response, *Oh well*, and asked myself that question, I began to take deliberate steps toward making the dream come true. What I finally learned is that just because I think something doesn't mean it's true.

What You Can Do

You, too, can ask yourself the question I asked myself, *What would it take to do it?* Your answers might include steps that seem daunting, but they will provide a practical place to start imagining solutions. In the art exhibit example above, the question "What would it take?" suggested the answers: frequent flyer tickets and a little vacation time.

You can also be more general in your questions. You can ask yourself:

What am I telling myself that might not be true?

And:

What habits of thinking are getting in my way?

Pay attention to whatever answers come to mind. Those answers might surprise you.

Henry Ford is credited with the saying "Whether you think you can, or you think you can't, you're right." In other words, if we think we can do something, that is real to us, and we probably can. And if we think we cannot do it, then *that* is our reality. Our thinking determines our belief, and we literally create our reality with our thinking. Our thoughts seem so real to us, we assume they *are* real and don't question them.

So in the quest to make your dreams come true, take this lesson to heart: Don't believe everything you think!

Try This: Don't Believe Everything You Think

Sometimes writing helps us understand our thoughts more clearly. Try writing your answers to these two sets of questions.

QUESTIONS SPECIFIC TO DREAMING
Think of something you'd really like to do, but think you can't.

1. What is it?

   _____
   _____
   _____

2. What are you thinking that might not be true?

   _____
   _____
   _____
   _____

3. What would it take to be able to do this?

   _____
   _____
   _____
   _____
   _____

4. If you can't see your way to doing this right now, what part of it might you do, or how might you prepare to do it in the future? Is there something similar, if less ambitious, you could do?

   _____
   _____
   _____
   _____

General Questions about Thinking

1. What habits of thinking get in your way, slow you down, or discourage you? In my case, for example, my habit of immediately thinking of reasons I couldn't do something and reasons why I was different from someone who could regularly got in my way.

_____

_____

_____

_____

2. Is there one habit of thinking you could change by noticing when you think it, catching yourself, and thinking something else? What is that habit, and how might you change it? For example, I changed the habit of immediately thinking of reasons I couldn't do something by noticing when I did it; slowing down by saying to myself, *Wait a minute*; and then asking, *What would it take to do it?*

_____

_____

_____

_____

Now Consider This: Noticing Is a Dreaming Skill

Noticing is one of six dreaming skills that have helped me recognize and realize my dreams. The skills are basic to all of the lessons, and I address them in

"Now Consider This" sections in this and other chapters where I think they will be most helpful to you. Like the lessons, the skills are developed over time, with practice. And like the lessons, they are related to each other; they overlap. These are the six dreaming skills:

- noticing
- relaxing
- listening
- choosing thoughtfully
- taking time
- living purposefully

First: noticing.

I *noticed* my disappointment and resignation over the San Francisco art show, caught my automatic thinking, and asked myself the question, What would it take? In doing so, I noticed, finally, that I was assuming, without really thinking, what I could or couldn't do. Noticing what I was feeling and thinking was an important step toward making choices and directing my life as I wanted to, not as other people might expect, or as most people might do. It took my strong yearning to see the Impressionist show to break through my knee-jerk thinking and believing.

You, too, can notice what you love. Notice what you are happiest doing. Notice how you feel when you picture yourself doing what you dream of doing. Don't censor yourself as you notice. You don't have to tell yourself that you can't, or it's too much, or other people wouldn't like it, or you don't deserve it. Forget all that for now, and give yourself a chance to notice and to recognize your dream.

Here's an exercise I call "Ask Little Abby." Every once in a while, sometimes when I'm driving alone in the car, I imagine the child in me—and after all there is one in each of us—sitting in the passenger seat beside me. I simply ask her, *How are you, Little Abby? How do you feel?* And Little Abby's answer often pops right into my mind. Sometimes I'm surprised, sometimes dismayed, but I get information. When I slow down and notice Little Abby, she helps me notice how I'm feeling and what I'm thinking *right now*, at a time when I may not have been noticing anything. I can also ask her, *What would you really like?* And again, she tells me. A side benefit of this exercise is that if little Abby says she is feeling nervous or afraid or unhappy for some reason, my grown-up self is able to assure her that I can take care of her and together we will be okay.

Try asking these questions of the child in you, using your name. You might be surprised at what you'll learn:

How are you?

How do you feel?

What would you really like?

Listen to her answers, and know that your grown-up self can take care of her.

You Deserve to Dream

Stay in the moment.
Recognize your dreams.
Relaxing is a dreaming skill.

I started sailing as a sophomore in college in Annapolis, Maryland, in 1962. The school owned a fleet of small boats, and I made time to sail down College Creek and out into the Chesapeake Bay during the long Maryland falls and springs. Later, at school in Madison, Wisconsin, I joined the Hoofers Outdoor Club and sailed on Lake Mendota. The club always had a boat available—one summer I dropped a course so I could sail more. I loved being away from the bustle of life and school and work, even on a city lake. I loved the motion of the boat, the sound of the wind, the look and whoosh of the bow wave as the boat cut through the water. And I loved how only the present moment counted—I wasn't aware of anything else.

After years of not sailing, and after my trip to the art show in San Francisco, a friend at work, Sandy, invited me to join her and her husband on board their sailboat. Sandy and John were members of a sailing club in Hudson, Wisconsin, and we sailed together on the St. Croix River. Soon Sandy and John

suggested that I join the club as an auxiliary member. I didn't need a boat; the only requirements were an interest in sailing and a small fee, and so I joined. I made new friends in the group and had many chances to sail in the quirky river winds. We would head south down the St. Croix, with the Minnesota shore to the west and Wisconsin to the east, stopping at sandbars to picnic and swim. Sometimes we'd raft up with other boats for potluck dinners, and then anchor overnight. We'd sail south until the river widened, becoming Lake Pepin, before we'd turn back. I enjoyed every moment on board.

With Sandy and John and other sailing club friends, I made three winter trips between 1987 and 1993 to islands in the Caribbean—welcome warm-weather escapes from the Minneapolis cold. On each trip we chartered a sailboat bareboat—that is, without professional crew. John, the most experienced sailor, was captain, and the rest of us were crew and followed John's directions. We spent our two-week holidays sailing among the islands—the British Virgin Islands, Guadeloupe and the Saints, Dominica, Grenada and the Grenadines—anchoring wherever we wished, swimming off the boat, soaking up the sunshine, napping in the cockpit, taking it easy. We enjoyed life on the islands too. Hiking park trails, finding the fresh markets, preparing local and sometimes unfamiliar foods, meeting craftspeople, learning island history, collecting souvenirs, and always, always, reveling in the pleasures of the water, the wind, and the sun. I loved every moment, and when it came time to return home at the end of each vacation, I could hardly stand to board the plane.

During our first trip, in the British Virgin Islands, we met a couple from Chicago who had retired early, sold their home and most of their possessions, and moved onto their sailboat. They traveled wherever they wanted to go and stayed as long as they liked. Their life was a revelation to me. I had never known anyone who lived that way. And in those relaxed, sunny moments of our meeting and talking, I knew I wanted to do exactly what they were doing. I recognized my dream and I yearned for it.

I was single at the time, in my forties, working. My son, Ben, had just started college, and I was nowhere near ready to retire. This was not a dream that would be within reach anytime soon, or maybe ever. But I told myself, *I get to have this dream, and I get to work toward realizing it.*

I began to prepare, to lay the groundwork for *the possibility* of realizing my dream. In the early 1990s, I took sailing lessons offered by the city's Parks and Recreation Department. For this first step, I went to Lake Calhoun in

Minneapolis at lunchtime twice a week for four weeks. In small sailing skiffs, I and the other students followed the direction of the instructor in the lead boat. We practiced sailing into the wind, at right angles to the wind, and off the wind. We learned how to come about, how to jibe, and how to control the speed of the boat by changing its angle to the wind. Lake Calhoun is surrounded by the city, but we could have been miles from town, it felt so freeing. Every moment was a pleasure.

Later, I splurged on a week's vacation to Marathon Key, Florida, taking a more advanced course on a larger boat with the Annapolis Sailing School. In the mid-'90s, I was able to buy an old twenty-four-foot sailboat—I named her *Abbycadabra*—and keep her in a little marina on Lake Superior, in northern Wisconsin. I knew I would never live alone on a sailboat and manage it myself, but owning a small boat made me more serious about becoming a competent sailor and more confident about my skills. I practiced, always with someone else on board, in calm weather on the big lake.

What I Learned: I Can Dream, and I Can Reach for My Dreams

Through my sailing experiences, I learned that I get to dream, even to dream big, and to work toward making my dreams come true. And I learned that staying in the present moment makes it not only possible but likely that I will recognize my dream and see ways to follow it.

We all deserve to dream, and move toward our dreams, no matter what they are. In my case, I yearned to live aboard a sailboat. Your dreams may be completely different. The point is you get to *notice* what you want, daydream about achieving it, and lay the groundwork for it. You don't have to be perfect. You don't have to have done anything spectacular. You don't have to prove that you deserve your dream. You can even feel worried or afraid or that you shouldn't want something. Even with those feelings, or in spite of them, you can *notice* what your dream is, watch for opportunities to prepare for it, and do what you can to move closer to making it come true.

You can recognize your dreams and prepare to make them come true, no matter what those dreams might be.

LESSON 2

My friend Julie learned this lesson when she noticed that she had been, as she says, "obsessing about retirement" for a year. Julie is a long-term, high-level administrator with a major health care provider. She kept asking herself, *Can I retire early? When can I retire? Can I survive another twenty-five years without working? What would I do if I left my current job?* Julie yearned to be more flexible with her time and do more of what she wanted to do. She assumed that she could achieve that only by retiring. And yet she wasn't financially ready for retirement.

Julie took my workshop and noticed, as she said, that she was stuck in her thinking and focusing more on the future than on the present. During the workshop, she slowed down, stayed focused on the moment, and realized that what she really wanted was more discretionary time. Perhaps she could change her thinking about work. In her words:

> I changed my attitude about work. I used to think I had to be at my desk between 7:45 and 5:00 (or 5:30 or 6:00) or I wasn't a good employee, that I would be perceived as not being committed to my job. Since the workshop I've been making an effort to leave by 5:00 at the latest, and some days at 4:30. I also am more relaxed about scheduling personal appointments during the day and rearranging my work schedule in order fit in more personal time.
>
> I could really see the difference in my thinking New Year's Day when my refrigerator broke. My immediate reaction was to look at my work schedule to see when was the earliest I didn't have anything scheduled at work, so I could stay home for the repairperson. That would have been four days later. I caught myself, noticed my thinking and instead decided to accept the first available time the repairperson had, which was the next day. I rescheduled a meeting, worked from home that day and didn't have to go four days without a refrigerator.
>
> I still get my work done, I just think about my job differently. I actually have freed up more time to do things I want to do. I also decided to take a three-week trip to South Africa, a trip that will combine two weeks of outreach work with my church and a week's safari, another dream. I've never been away from work that long except while on maternity leave, thirty years ago!

I'm more present now, and as I notice how I spend my time differently, I see that other people do a better job than I do of balancing personal time with work time. As I do more of that balancing, I like my job better and feel more relaxed about not needing an immediate escape plan from working full time.

What You Can Do

Staying in the moment is a prerequisite for *noticing* thoughts, feelings, surroundings, and *what you would really love to do.*

If you are busy planning or remembering, you can't be in touch with yourself in the here and now. And if you're not in touch with yourself in the present, you can't recognize your deepest wishes, because just as we can't be in two places at once physically, we can't be in two places mentally or emotionally. To the extent that your mind is busy thinking about what happened yesterday or what might happen tomorrow, you can't recognize what you're thinking and feeling right now. And to the extent that you're operating on autopilot as you carry out your everyday responsibilities, you can't notice what your reactions are in the present moment. Staying in the moment is key to noticing, and noticing is key to recognizing and reaching for your dreams.

Try This: Stay in the Moment

In this simple exercise you use your senses to ground yourself in the present moment. So make yourself a cup of tea or a cold drink, settle yourself comfortably, take a few deep breaths, and begin. The first two instructions are about identifying what you see and hear; these may be the easiest. Take your time, and try them all.

1. Quietly look around you. What are ten things that you see now?
2. Close your eyes now, and listen. What are five sounds that you hear?
3. Use your nose. What odors can you identify?
4. Now notice taste. What taste or tastes do you recognize?

5. Now notice your sense of touch. What are you touching, or what is touching you? Do you feel the air, your clothing? What you are sitting on? Identify connections with your sense of touch.

Using our senses to come back to the present can put us in touch with thoughts and feelings as well. Now answer these questions:

How do you feel?

What are you thinking?

What are your insights?

You can do this short exercise any time you want to bring yourself to the present moment. Using your senses deliberately to notice what is around you helps you center yourself. And that helps put you in touch with your present thoughts and feelings. That connection, in turn, can lead you to new insights.

Now Consider This: Relaxing Is a Dreaming Skill

The Stay in the Moment exercise is the first of several in this book intended to help you slow down and relax, and that is because no one relaxes once and for all. Rather, we need to remind ourselves to relax and practice relaxing. Relaxing will help you stay in the present moment and stay in touch with yourself. And being in touch with yourself is necessary for dreaming at every stage, from beginning to understand what you really love to making your dream come true.

Our whole culture pushes against our relaxing. Instead, we are encouraged to speed up, fitting too much activity into too little time. We multitask, thinking that's something positive, and miss the satisfaction that comes from focusing on doing one thing at a time and doing it well. We want what we want right now, and patience and tolerance—for others and ourselves—get lost in the rush.

There are so many aids to relaxing. We all know what they are: physical exercise, a healthy diet, enough sleep, meditation and stress management practices, good friends. Some of the exercises in this book, like the Stay in the Moment exercise, will help you relax.

Whatever you are currently doing to help yourself, know that relaxation practices can help you recognize and reach for your dreams. And if you have not included such strategies regularly in your life, please begin without delay. They are not just for other people. They *will* pay off, and you'll be glad.

I do at least one thing every day specifically to relax. Okay, almost every day. The activity varies. It might be simply taking a walk in my neighborhood, or going for a bike ride. I read a meditation book. I get together with friends, and we laugh. I go to the gym, where I start with an aerobic exercise, do stretches, and then do weight-bearing exercises. Whatever I choose, it's something that takes me out of myself, and although I may think I don't have the time for it, the increase in my energy more than makes up for the time I spend. I suggest that you do the same: one relaxing exercise or event each day, designed to help you ease up.

So what will they be? Write your answers here:

_____

_____

_____

_____

_____

Here is a little breathing exercise to help you relax. You can do this any place, any time. Simply breathe in through your nose to a slow count of five, and then breathe out through your nose to a slow count of five. Repeat ten times, or until you notice that you feel more balanced.

You Already Have What You Need

Let your thinking flow.
Ask for what you want.
Do your homework.
Listening is a dreaming skill.

In the spring of 1984, I lost my job on the toss of a coin.

For the previous five years, I had been working for a state government agency that provided services and goods to small, mainly rural school districts. The districts could hire services on a cooperative basis, through seventeen agency branches around the state. Working at one of the branches, I wrote grants for monies available to districts for programs outside of the normal academic subjects and implemented those programs in the schools. One of my projects, for example, was to secure grant funds to develop alcohol and drug education programs for students in nine school districts and then implement those programs. (It was this work that led me to understand my husband's alcoholism.) Another project was to introduce a positive peer pressure program for upper elementary school kids. The projects were developed with the help of school teachers, counselors, administrators, and parents, and programming included components for parents. Much of the grant money

LESSON 3

went for training school staff to keep the programs going after the funding period was over.

I liked the job for its potential to help kids and their families and for its variety. I liked the people I worked with, including school staff and community members who helped develop the programs, and the teachers, counselors, and students who participated in them after we got the grants.

At the end of the 1983–1984 school year, the state legislature reduced the number of agency branches from seventeen to twelve, and our office was to be combined with another. The two branch directors, long-time school administrators and friends, decided to flip a coin to see who would continue as agency director. My boss lost the coin toss, and so did his staff. It was a difficult time for me: I lost my job, and my husband moved out during the very same week.

So I was a newly single mom in the summer of 1984, when my son was fifteen. Although I did have paid work for one day a week during the following school year, Ben and I couldn't get by on that. I felt great pressure to earn a living, though I certainly wasn't in good shape to go job hunting.

Losing my job was a setback I never wanted to repeat. While I thought about what to do immediately, two ideas niggled at me. One was that the only sure way not to lose another job on the toss of a coin or any other way was to work for myself. But how could I do that? What could I offer? The second thought was that, while I had always worked for public and nonprofit organizations, I was curious about the private sector and longed to try working there.

I started my homework. To learn more about private sector work, I began a series of informational interviews, first with people I knew who were working in business, then with people they knew, and so on. My goal in those conversations was to answer two questions: How could I make the change to private sector employment? What work might I like to do and be able to do there? Many people I spoke with discouraged me from trying to make the change, saying that business people generally did not hire teachers and other public sector employees. And although I worried that they might be right, deep down I didn't see why my experience should hinder me. It seemed to me that my skills could transfer to many different environments. I could organize information efficiently, write and speak effectively, and had teaching experience with children and adults. I thought I might already have the skills to do what I wished.

After months of informational interviewing, searching, and job interviews, during which time Ben thought I was going to drive us into the poorhouse,

I got a chance. I had spoken with the human resources director at a large Twin Cities corporation. That conversation resulted, as they all did, in his giving me the name of someone else to talk to and my sending him a thank-you note. I followed up on his leads and continued my informational interviewing, following each lead given me by every person I talked with.

About six weeks after our conversation, the HR director called to say he had an interesting possibility for me. His company's director of transportation was looking to hire someone on a limited-term, contract basis. The job was to teach the heads of the company's diesel mechanic shops and warehouse operations across the country how to use equipment tracking and maintenance software developed just for them. I knew nothing about software—this was 1985—but the director didn't want a techie to do the job. The folks who ran the warehouses and the diesel shops kept information about their equipment in their heads and in paper files, and they were skeptical of, if not downright hostile to, computers. This director didn't want an intimidating expert to work with them; he wanted someone who was willing to learn the software and able to teach. He thought if I kept half a step ahead of the folks I worked with, together we would learn to use and trust the software. He hired me.

Working in the company divisions around the country until everyone involved had been trained, I completed the project in two years. In fact, it was this work-related travel that led to the frequent flyer tickets that led to the art show I told you about in the first lesson. I never worried about being able to do the work. In spite of the discouragement I had gotten from others, I had all the skills I needed, including the skill to recognize when I had to learn something new, and the stick-to-itiveness to do that. And I found the job by doing my homework.

It wasn't my dream job, but I worked hard and learned what software could do—I actually wrote documentation for much of it, learning in the process how time-consuming that is, and why so much software is poorly documented. I made a good living and accomplished the change from public to private sector work. That two-year project was the first long stride toward my dream job. The job got me into the private sector and set me back on my feet financially. Now I was ready for the next step. Exactly what that would be, I had no idea.

Toward the end of the software project, I began informational interviewing again to explore opportunities and figure out what I would like to do next and what was possible. During that process, the same HR director who had called

two years before referred me to a director he knew in the research group at a Minneapolis-based training and consulting firm. That firm specialized in people skills: management and leadership, sales and customer service, negotiating and communication. The HR director also said he thought if I wanted to work for a training and consulting firm, I would have to begin at an entry level, for much lower pay than I was getting at the time. Discouraging news. But I had heard that kind of message before. I was forty-three years old, and I didn't let his warning stop me.

The director at the training company talked with me about his organization and gave me a tour, including peeks into training seminars in session at the time. I saw how the seminar facilitators and the groups interacted, heard their laughter, noticed the colorful flipcharts posted on the walls. The energy of the sessions pulled me in, and I fell in love with the company. They weren't hiring—I found out later there had been a recent layoff—and anyway I thought there was no way they would hire me. I certainly didn't have the right résumé. I wondered what I could do to continue my association with the company—if nothing else, I was eager to take one of their courses—and decided to sleep on it. The next morning, relaxed after a good night's sleep, I had an idea.

I called the director in the research group and told him I would like to take one of the leadership courses the company offered. The courses were expensive, paid for by the employers of the people who took them. I asked him if there were something I could do for the company—a project I could do as a volunteer in exchange for taking a course. Believe it or not, he said yes.

For the volunteer project, I interviewed company salespeople by telephone about their successes with clients and wrote up the interviews. I worked in a small office the director provided, so I was right where I wanted to be. Soon after I started, I took a seminar; I was amazed at my enthusiasm for it, and I admired the facilitator, wished I could be up there where he was, and wondered how I could make that happen.

While I was in the building working on my project and taking the class, I talked with employees in the hallways, in the lunchroom, wherever I could, and got to know quite a few of them. At the end of the interviewing project, the research guy gave me a bit of paid work, writing parts of a training manual. A little later, he asked me to travel to Chicago to sit in on a new program that, unusually, had no ready training materials. He wanted to develop manuals for the new program for both seminar leaders and participants, and he asked me to help him.

In Chicago for those few days, I attended the seminar, took copious notes, and conferred with my colleague. I also met the account manager for the seminar client. After several conversations with this account manager during the time I was there, she suggested I call her boss. She said they needed someone like me in their office, to tailor seminars to individual clients and to teach the seminars. I called the boss, and we talked by phone. A few weeks later that boss was in Minneapolis. She met with me and, after a half-hour interview, hired me. I learned later that after our phone conversation in Chicago, she had asked around the company about me. Having done my homework by meeting and talking with company employees, I had gotten good press.

In September 1988, just after my son began his sophomore year in college, I moved to Chicago for my dream job, my dream boss, and a higher salary than I had ever made. During my first week there, I celebrated my forty-fifth birthday.

My three years of employment with the consulting company, before it was sold and reorganized, set me up to start my own little consulting business back in Minneapolis. In early 1992, eight years after losing my job on the toss of a coin, I did just that, thus fulfilling my dream of working for myself.

What I Learned: I Already Have What I Need

I learned four important dreaming lessons over those eight years while I was getting my dream job:

1. Know that I have what I need to do what I want to do, even if whatever it is at first seems out of reach.
2. Relax and let my thinking flow. Pushing my mind—bearing down on the problem—doesn't produce results. Creative ideas come from a relaxed mind.
3. Do my homework. Be imaginative about learning what I need to know about the path toward reaching my dream, and do the research.

4. Ask for what I want. When I realize what I need, or want, I get to ask someone for help, and that person gets to say yes or no.

Those lessons are continually reinforced for me, and they apply to you too. The next section, What You Can Do (page 24), has specific suggestions for you to try.

Here are the four lessons again, one at a time.

Know That I Have What I Need

You and I have everything we need, deep inside, to create and follow our dreams. That doesn't mean that we might not have to learn something, or prepare in some way, for what we want. When learning and preparation are necessary, we'll realize it.

What keeps us from recognizing and following a dream isn't something we don't have, something that's missing. Rather, what gets in the way is the extra stuff that swirls around our minds: *It will never happen. I could never do it. It would cost too much. There's no time. I'm too young. I'm too old. My family won't like it. What will people think? I've got kids. I'm too busy.* The task here is to notice our thinking, remind ourselves that just because we think it doesn't mean it's true, deliberately sweep those thoughts away, and replace them with the understanding that we have everything we need.

Relax and Let My Thinking Flow

When we let go of all that tension-producing mental static, we can relax and let our thinking flow. And when we do that—when we don't press, judge, object to, or argue with ourselves—then our wisest, most creative, and best thinking happens. We get out of our own way, and our genius appears.

Many elements that, over time, helped make my dream job come true were involved in my relaxed, free-flowing thought. These elements included inspiration for ideas along the way, recognition of what would be helpful, confidence to take initiative, the continuing work of improving my craft at each job, recognition and appreciation of other people's help, and picking myself up after setbacks.

Do My Homework

Making dreams come true involves homework. Some people may have good fortune dropped in their laps, but most of us pave our own way. And that's the lesson: homework paves the way for good luck. (For more on the importance of homework, see Lesson 5, Do Your Homework, Consider Trade-Offs, Then Decide.)

In getting my dream job my homework included asking people to talk with me and preparing for the interviews by learning what I could about the company where the interviewee worked. It included the interviews themselves. I went into each one with five things in mind I wanted to know about them and five things I wanted them to know about me. It included making sure I left each interview with a new lead, either in the same company or a different one, and following up with a thank-you note. I did my very best completing the volunteer project at the consulting company where I knew I wanted to work, and I met and talked with many people there. Much of my homework was enjoyable—I remember wishing someone would pay me to do those informational interviews! *What a great job that would be,* I thought. But no one did, and I did the homework not knowing what the outcome would be. I reminded myself to trust that my homework would pay off.

Ask for What I Want

Sometimes we're reluctant to ask for what we need or want. Maybe we feel shy, or don't want to impose, or we hope someone will guess what we need, or it seems unreasonable to want whatever it is. But I've found that often people are happy to grant a request. Benjamin Franklin said, "He that has once done you a Kindness will be more ready to do you another, than he whom you yourself have obliged."

Sometimes people you ask for help, like my contact at the consulting company, see the request as an opportunity for themselves. Volunteering at his company was interesting for me, and it was very helpful to him. Providing me with the seminar was easy for him, and it meant a lot to me.

Asking for help shows people that you are human, that you aren't able to do absolutely everything by yourself. In other words, it shows that you are more like them!

Don't be afraid to ask. You might be surprised at how pleased the other person is to accommodate your request. Be sure to ask in a way that makes it easy for the other person to say no; in other words, be sure that you are making a request and not a demand. And be ready to accept the answer, whatever it is, with good grace, with pleased thanks if your request is granted, and a pleasant manner and understanding words if it is not.

What You Can Do

Here are some specific suggestions for you for each of the four lessons.

First, Know That You Have What You Need

If you are thinking something is impossible, if you're thinking you don't know an answer or you wouldn't know where to start something, remember Lesson 1: Just because you think something doesn't mean it's true. Then you can ask yourself these questions:

> What would I do if I thought this were possible?
>
> What would I say if I knew the answer?
>
> Where would I start if I knew where to start?

For example, when I wanted to change from public sector to private sector work, many people told me about how difficult it would be to do so unless I started at an entry level, thus taking a large pay cut. I asked myself, *What would I do if I thought this move were possible, and such a job would pay me an acceptable salary?* My answer was: *I would talk to people who are doing things that I might like to do, in private sector settings that interest me.*

And that's what I did.

Try asking yourself whichever question fits the dream you want to fulfill. You might be doubly surprised, first that you come up with an answer, and then at what the answer is!

Second, Relax and Let Your Thinking Flow

Notice when your mind is busy, distracted, even racing. When it's like that, your thinking will not be easy or intuitive. What gets in the way of our recognizing our wishes, of tapping into the natural wisdom we all have inside us, isn't something that's missing. It's the mental static we generate. We need to slow down our busy minds and clear out the static so our thinking can flow.

Once you notice that your mind is racing, you can either put off important thinking that requires your creativity or begin to release those busy thoughts and replace them with the knowledge that you have exactly the right mind and heart now to move toward your dream. Here is an analogy that illustrates this idea:

> Imagine a swimming pool, calm in the morning sun. No one is there yet, for the day has just begun. All is quiet. Now imagine the pool a few hours later. The lifeguards are on duty, moms and dads occupy the chairs around the pool, little kids are wading in the shallow end, and big kids are jumping and diving into the deep water. Everyone is swimming and splashing, enjoying the cool, wet break in the hot day. The water in the pool is no longer calm. It's choppy, splashy, and noisy. And yet the tranquility of the pool isn't lost. All it will take to restore the water to its natural calm is for the swimmers to get out of the pool.

It's the same with us. When we slow down, when one by one those swimmers leave the pool, we can quietly and calmly listen to ourselves.

Sometimes it's not as easy to calm a busy mind as it is to imagine getting swimmers out of a pool. You might notice that your mind is busy and not be able right then to let go of those racing thoughts. They might continue to dog you against your will. Okay, it happens. This is the time for the exercise, meditation, or whatever stress-reducing strategies help you. And it's the time for patience.

You know that when you're tense, your thinking is not at its best. In fact, that very tension is an indicator that it's not at its best. And from that lower-quality thinking come doubts and shaky confidence. Low-quality thinking generates discouragement and reasons you can't do something. So don't believe yourself right then; don't believe what you're thinking. Wait until you are relaxed, until the swimmers are out of the pool.

When your mood lifts, your thinking will calm, and your reality will look different to you. Give yourself a chance to listen deeply to yourself, to tap into your own wisdom. You'll find it when your thoughts stop racing and your low mood lifts.

Here's an example. My friend Nancy had had a long-distance relationship for seven years—the two had met online—when she and Art decided to get married. As they told friends and family about their engagement, they were inundated with questions about where they would live, and as they got closer to their wedding, those questions got more pressing. Nancy and Art grew more tense as they felt they had to make a decision. But they both had young adult children and elderly moms in or near their respective cities, Minneapolis and Portland. Art's job involved a lot of travel, so he wasn't home that much anyway, and he generally had a large stash of frequent flyer miles, so they saw each other often. One evening at dinner they were talking about the dilemma with Tom and me. We pointed out that they already had a relationship that worked for them. They were getting married, and Nancy was about to retire, and that's plenty of change for one year. Just because other people were pressing them with questions was no reason why they had to make a decision, and just because others might make a more conventional decision was no reason they had to follow suit.

Nancy and Art breathed a sigh of relief, as if they had gotten permission to relax about it, and that was the end of that. After two years of marriage they maintain her house in Minneapolis and his condo in Portland, and that's working great. They can make a different decision if and when they're ready, and they can do that from the same place they came from when they relaxed and decided not to let other people's ideas determine their choices. They got the swimmers out of the pool, and the water calmed.

Third, Do Your Homework

In a calm moment, ask yourself what you need to know, or do, to begin down the path toward your dream. Are there people who have knowledge or experience in the area of your interest, whom you might talk with? Is there information online or at the library that would be helpful? Which of your own experiences will help you here?

As you do your homework and understand more of what your dream involves, don't be discouraged by what might appear as an obstacle. There will be some obstacles, and you will have to deal with them, but not right now. This is the time to do your homework, gather information, get the big picture. You can—and will—narrow things down later.

How about doing a little homework right now? Here are some simple suggestions:

- Is there someplace you would like to go? Alaska, perhaps, or Rome? Find out what the schedule and fares would be if you were to go by plane, train, bus, or boat. Or, if applicable, what it would take to drive there.
- Is there something you would like to try doing? Rock climbing, for example? If there is someone you know who's a rock climber, call that person and find out more about it. Or go online to find out where there is a climbing opportunity near you.
- Is there something you would like to learn? Better use of kitchen knives, for example? Call a kitchen store near you to see if they offer classes. Or bridge? Is there a bridge club in your town? Find out, and give them a call.

In these and similar, simple ways, you can begin.

Fourth, Ask for What You Want

Are you reluctant to do this? Perhaps you value self-sufficiency and think you *should* be able to do everything yourself. But when you ask, you give yourself a chance not only to get help but also to make a connection with someone who might see your request as an opportunity. Once, after a romantic disappointment, I asked friends for company so I wouldn't be alone. I was busy and distracted at work during the week, but Saturdays and Sundays were tough, as I kept thinking about the man who left. Friends were happy to oblige on several successive weekends, and my spirits lifted. And they told me they had never thought of asking for help before, but felt freer to do so after I asked them.

Another example: when my friend Nancy—the same wise friend in the story above—was undergoing difficult medical treatments, she asked for help

cleaning her basement. She was not happy with the condition of the basement but didn't have the energy to tackle the cleanup. Six of us showed up on a Saturday and made an enjoyable day—and short work—of the project. Some of us took home things Nancy no longer needed, and that was a bonus.

Sometimes the person you ask will decline. You can assure the person that it's fine, and ask someone else.

Not every request for or offer of help leads to fulfilling a dream. But by all means, look for opportunities to ask for what you want—you never know where it might lead.

To practice, think of something you'd like to know, or something you'd like help with. Now think of one or two people who might have an answer or be able to help. Call one of them and ask, and just see what happens.

Try This: Belly Breathing

Here's another breathing exercise to help you relax. I include it here because relaxing is the beginning and the basis of all other dreaming activities. The exercise is called Diaphragmatic Breathing, or Belly Breathing.

1. Sit or lie down comfortably, removing tight clothing and any other distractions or encumbrances.
2. Put one hand flat over your belly and your other hand flat on your chest.
3. Breathe in slowly and deeply through your nose, pushing your belly out as you do so, to bring the air down into it, as far down as you can. Keep your chest and shoulders as still as possible—the hand on your chest should not move.
4. When you have taken in as much air as you can, blow it out very slowly through your mouth. If you can, take about twice as long to exhale as you did to inhale.
5. Rest briefly and repeat: Breathe in slowly and deeply through your nose, pushing your belly out and keeping your chest and shoulders as still as possible. And again breathe out slowly through your mouth.
6. Keep breathing that way, in slowly and deeply through your nose, out even more slowly through your mouth. Notice that your belly

  expands and contracts as you do so, and your chest and shoulders remain still.
7. Focus on your breathing as you do the exercise. After some moments, you'll notice your body settling down, and you'll feel relaxed.

Don't get discouraged if you don't feel that sense of relaxation right away. When I started belly breathing, it took me about ten minutes to relax. Gradually, as I practiced once or twice each day, I found that I relaxed more quickly and easily, and needed just a few minutes.

When you find you are able to do the belly breathing fairly easily, try focusing on a single word, like a mantra, as you breathe. That focus will further help you relax. If you're like me, the more you belly breathe, the more relaxed you will be.

The step from a relaxed state of mind to an insight is not automatic or rational. Insights come to us out of the blue, without preparation and without logical thought. We can't will them into being by dint of concentration. And yet we all have the capacity for those insights, if we are willing to slow down, listen to ourselves, and let the insights come.

I have learned to be patient and trust that at some point when my mind is calm, the wisdom I need, the insight I'm hoping for, will appear. Sometimes my insight suggests something large, a general direction or goal. And sometimes it suggests something specific, like learning a skill or laying groundwork. Whatever the size or nature of the insights, if we trust our own wisdom, those insights will help lead us to our dreams.

Now Consider This: Listening Is a Dreaming Skill

I never realized how important listening was until I met Jared in 1981. Jared is the best listener I have ever met. I knew him for only ten days and haven't seen him since—it's been well over thirty years now. And yet, when I think about listening, I picture Jared.

Jared was a river rat, a professional whitewater rafting guide. That year, nine members of our extended family took a raft trip down the Middle Fork of

the Salmon River in Idaho. Johnny, a family friend and professional river guide, organized and led the trip. Family members included me, my husband, and our son, then twelve; two of his cousins (nine and twelve) and their parents; and another aunt and uncle. Completing our party of fourteen were Johnny, his girlfriend, Diane, and three of Johnny's river guide friends, including Jared. We had four rafts. Johnny captained the paddle raft, and six of us were his crew. At his direction, we paddled our way downstream, stopping to scout rapids before going through them. The other rafts, rowed by the three other river rats, held our camping equipment, luggage, food, the children, and whichever adult wasn't paddling just then.

Jared was unusual in several ways. Lean and independent, he didn't eat the same food as the rest of us, carrying instead ingredients for his vegetarian, mostly raw diet and growing sprouts in a cloth bag over the side of his raft. He said he had recently started paying attention to—*noticing*—how he felt after meals, and he altered what and how much he ate accordingly. He was gradually adjusting his diet as he made his discoveries. In camp, Jared wore moccasins he had hand-stitched, and he was sewing a soft, loose shirt during our trip. He said these garments were more comfortable than other clothes, and making them himself was satisfying. Jared challenged himself professionally by taking the most difficult routes through the Middle Fork's frequent rapids; he said it honed his river skills.

In other words, Jared listened carefully to himself, adjusting his diet, his clothing, and the way he did his work according to the insights and understanding he gained. Listening to ourselves using this kind of undivided attention is how we recognize and begin to see our way clear to recognizing and reaching for our dreams.

In my own case, as much pressure as I felt to go to work after I lost my job on the toss of a coin, by listening to myself I understood that I did not want to go back to classroom teaching. I had very much enjoyed my seven years in the classroom, but I knew, deep down, that I was hungry for a new experience. Another logical choice at that time would have been school administration. I had the teaching and the staff-training experience that was good preparation for administration, and I could have gotten the necessary certification. Very logical, and yet as I listened quietly to myself, I knew I did not want to follow that path.

The connection is clear between listening to yourself and recognizing what you really want, as Jared did and as I did. I believe there is also a connection between listening to others and pursuing your dreams. Here is more of Jared's story.

In conversation with others, Jared listened as intently as he listened to himself. When he talked with you, he was all yours. Nothing distracted him.

One evening, Jared and I were sitting on a stone ledge above the water. The rapids below crashed and boomed. In camp behind us, the kids were running and hollering and playing, and the adults on KP were setting up the kitchen, clattering, calling to each other, getting dinner ready. Yet around the two of us there was calm. Jared was relaxed and focused. His eyes met mine, but he didn't stare. He was still, with an interested expression on his face, and I could feel his presence and attention. When he spoke, he remained relaxed, low-key. Our conversation was effortless. It seemed as if the sky could be falling and Jared would still be focused. That evening we talked about noticing, about how much understanding comes to you if you are attentive, and how that attentiveness can be life changing. I noticed how attentive Jared was to me—I had rarely been listened to in the way he was listening. Reciprocating, I listened to him equally intently. Later I wondered how often I had listened to someone with such steady, quiet focus. Jared's influence led me to practice that kind of listening, to others and to myself, beginning right away. I wasn't as good at it as he was, but I've gotten better, and Jared is still influencing me, all these years later.

Others in that long-ago group also recognized how satisfying it was to talk with Jared. We were all drawn to him, adults and children alike, and we vied for his attention. We told him more than we were inclined to tell someone who didn't listen as well, and he no doubt gained a more nuanced knowledge of each of us. I, and perhaps others too, appreciated the unusual gift he offered, the genuine connection we made and the depth of understanding that came from our conversations.

I believe that careful listening is often reciprocal: when someone listens intently to me, as Jared did, I am more likely to listen fully to him. That reciprocal, careful listening leads to better, more intimate relationships and indeed is an important basis for a good relationship. Those good relationships foster a fuller exchange of ideas, better understanding, more hope and confidence, and the likelihood of more mutual help as we discover our dreams and begin to make them come true. The connection between careful listening to others and dreaming is not as direct as the connection between listening to yourself and dreaming, but it's there.

My friend Priscilla credits the realization of her dreams of travel in part to conversations she's had with friends. She and her husband had travelled, but after he died, she was reluctant to do so on her own. And yet she dreamed of going to Africa to see the animals, and especially the giraffes, in their natural habitat. Priscilla says:

> When I returned to Minnesota from my two years in Madison, I ran into Sue, a friend from my previous church community. She asked what I had been doing, and I replied, "It's not what I have been doing but what I want to do that's important. I want to go to Africa and see giraffes run in the wild." Serendipity and the universe answered. Sue was booked on a trip to Tanzania led by Jim Klobuchar, who wrote for the *Star Tribune* for many years. Right then and there, Sue's listening and sharing made my dream come true. I signed up for that trip, too, and Sue and I roomed together in tents with baboons leaping in the trees above and in old hunting camps in the Rift Valley. I did, indeed, get to see giraffes in their native habitat, eating acacia trees. Giraffes fear nothing, as one thrust of their hooves can level any animal that threatens, so, rather than running, they meander. This was the trip of a lifetime for me, and since then I have hatched other travel dreams.

Here is one more story, with a different link to listening. It's from my friend Julie, the same woman who changed how she thinks about work. Here are her words:

> My experience with listening intently and achieving a goal goes back to when I ran the Twin Cities Marathon. I had been running for a while and competing in 10K races. I use the term "competing" loosely because for me it was a race to finish, not anything else. The afternoon/evening after a 10K race I was at my parents' 50th wedding anniversary and ran into Lorelei, the daughter of good friends of theirs and someone I knew from childhood but never really socialized with as an adult, even though we are the same age. We got to talking about running and she said to me, "You could run the Twin Cities Marathon." I thought she was nuts. She had completed five marathons, and

invited me to run with a group of women she routinely trained with. I thought, *I'll just run with them.* Lorelei became my coach. She told me how to train, and always said, "You can do this." I listened to her, not really believing her. After I had run a couple of long runs with her, I began to think maybe I could run a marathon. I finally talked to my dad about getting a race number, which the race director gave me because he knew my dad—the course was full by that time. I still didn't tell anyone I was really training for the marathon because I wasn't convinced I could do it. But Lorelei continued to tell me I could. And she was right, because I did.

Four Kinds of Listening

Here are descriptions of four different kinds of listening. These helped me to become more deliberate about the way I listen, and I hope they do the same for you.

Not many of us listen the way Jared did—to ourselves or to others. Most of us listen in a distracted way, in a judgmental way, or in a tensely focused way to make sure we get every word. And yet we all have the opportunity to listen in the relaxed, undivided way that Jared did, the way that's a gift to ourselves and to the speaker.

DISTRACTED LISTENING

When we listen in a distracted way, we are thinking of four or five other things at the same time. This *distracted* listening is hard on the brain, which has to stay busy to keep up. And the result of distracted listening is that nothing gets the attention it deserves. Busy parents sometimes listen to their young children in this way. The children register their dissatisfaction by putting their little hands on the parent's face, turning it toward themselves, looking into the parent's eyes and saying, "Dad, Dad."

JUDGMENTAL LISTENING

Or we listen in a *judgmental* way, pigeonholing parts of what the speaker says: *Oh, I don't agree with that at all*, we think, or, *She should talk with so-and-so about that*, or, *We've tried that before, and it didn't work.* And while we're busy judging and pigeonholing, we miss some of the specifics and much of the

overall message. This kind of listening also keeps our brains working hard but doesn't allow us to give our full attention to the speaker.

Tensely Focused Listening

While practicing *tensely focused* listening, we may busily write down everything the speaker says, so we'll be sure not to miss anything. This is a good way to listen when someone is giving us directions to a place we've never been, and college students sometimes take class notes this way. But if the person talking suddenly says something really, really important, or something startling or especially interesting, many of us note takers put down our pens and, at last, give our full attention to the speaker.

Then we listen in the fourth way: relaxed, undivided listening.

Relaxed, Undivided Listening

Relaxed, undivided listening is the calm, quiet, fully focused listening Jared practiced. It is low-effort, for we have slowed down. Our brains are relaxed. It is high-impact, as we take in the speaker's whole message: words, tone, and body language. The speaker, in turn, is fully aware of our undivided listening.

Listening to ourselves using relaxed, undivided listening is how we reach our inner selves, our inner wisdom. And then we are able to recognize and begin to see our way clear to reaching for our dreams. When we listen to others using undivided listening, we give them the gift of listening, as Jared gave my family and me all those years ago. We create stronger connections with others and through those connections learn more deeply about them and about ourselves.

Try This: Notice and Practice Listening

First, spend some time just noticing how you are listening. Identify times when you're listening in a distracted way, a judgmental way, a tensely focused way—perhaps you're taking notes—and a relaxed, undivided way. Don't worry about how you're listening; don't criticize yourself. Just notice.

Then choose a time when you will listen to someone in the relaxed, undivided way I described above. Give the speaker your full, quiet, calm attention. Notice when your mind wanders, as it may well do. Simply bring your attention back to the speaker. And when your mind wanders again, bring your attention back again. Don't worry about it, and don't criticize yourself. No matter how many times your mind wanders, simply notice that it's happening and come back to the speaker.

You might be tempted, while the person is talking, to ask a question. Don't. You've probably noticed that when you do interrupt with a question, the speaker is likely to say, "I'm getting to that." Let her tell her story in her own way, organizing her own thoughts. If, at the end, you have a question, by all means ask it. And if you've forgotten your question in the meantime, let it go. Your relaxed, undivided listening is more important.

Or you might be tempted to interrupt the speaker with a similar story of your own, believing it will make a connection or reassure the speaker that you understand. Or you may think that when you don't say anything, the speaker will think you're not interested. But when you interrupt with your own story, you turn the conversation from a focus on her to a focus on yourself, stealing the attention the speaker thought she had. When you are listening in a relaxed, undivided way, you can let the speaker finish, taking in her whole message, giving her the gift of your relaxed, undivided listening. And then you can take your turn.

You might feel uncomfortable listening in this way. It might be unfamiliar. You might think that when you don't speak, there is no conversation. I urge you to try it, and try it again. Look for times when you're willing to give someone your relaxed, undivided listening. You'll become more comfortable as you do.

In talking about listening, after describing relaxed, undivided listening, I've sometimes asked people, "Who listens to you that way?" And often the answer has been: "My dog." For your family and friends, you can change that.

Some Dreams Are Impossible—
But They Are Clues

Grand dreams can serve as direction finders to smaller dreams.
Concentrate on what you *can* do something about, not on what you *can't*.

I've always wanted to have a good singing voice, and I just don't. When I wanted to sing in my high school choir and tried out, the director turned me down. "You have a sweet voice," she said. "But no." And friends have noticed, over the years, that I'm sometimes out of tune when I sing along with the car radio.

None of that stops me. I sing all the time, and I know the words to hundreds of songs. My favorites are American jazz and Broadway show tunes of the 1920s, '30s, '40s, and '50s—my mom and dad's music. I love Ella Fitzgerald, Billie Holiday, Nat King Cole, Satchmo. I know by heart Cole Porter tunes, Rodgers and Hart, Irving Berlin, the Gershwins, all the Tin Pan Alley greats. I attend musical theater and live jazz performances. I had the tremendous pleasure, twice, of hearing Ella Fitzgerald live in concert, once in a stadium and once up close in the third row at St. Paul's Ordway Theater.

It's really too bad I can hardly carry a tune, and it's getting worse as I get older, though my tunefulness still improves in the shower. Luckily, my husband enjoys my singing and encourages me—not that I need encouraging. Some years ago, I took voice lessons, and while my range grew slightly and I learned how to breathe, overall I didn't improve much. I might have gotten better if I had kept taking lessons, but I gave up.

It's clear that I'm not going to realize the dream of being a terrific singer. I'm thinking, *Perhaps in my next life, if there is such, I'll have the voice I long for.* And while I'm longing, I'd like to be a natural redhead as well. Of course, I could dye my hair red now, but I don't have the rest of the coloring to go with it, and anyway it's *natural* red hair I want. Oh well.

What I Learned: Some Dreams Are Impossible

Although some people say otherwise, we can't be whatever we want to be, have whatever we want to have, or do whatever we want to do. Some dreams, like my red-headed jazz singer dreams, are unrealistic, impossible. So I continue to sing around the house and enjoy listening to my favorite singers. And as far as natural red hair goes, I admire it on others.

I must distinguish between a dream I *can* do something about and a dream I *can't*. I don't want to spend precious energy on anything that is out of my control. I can take singing lessons and probably improve my voice, I can dye my hair red, but there is absolutely nothing I can do about the voice or the hair color I was born with. The way I was born will have to do. And you know what? It is good enough.

I'd rather concentrate on changes I can make, on things I can influence and bring into being.

Distinguishing between the possible and the impossible is not always easy. And the further a wish is from what we have already experienced, the more difficult, even impossible, it may seem to fulfill. So how do we determine what is and what is not possible?

There's no single, quick answer, but there are ways to address the question. One way is to ask myself my favorite questions:

What do I think is in my way?

What would it take to do this?

Here are some other helpful questions:

What about this dream appeals to me?

What are some related interests or activities I could pursue?

How can I capture some elements of a big dream, while relinquishing others?

Sometimes beginning smaller gives us confidence to dream bigger or suggests a related direction that may not be so daunting.

What You Can Do

Grand dreams, even impossible ones, are helpful, for they serve as direction finders and guideposts to smaller dreams, to living the way you really want to live and doing what you really want to do. Unfortunately, many of us, perhaps including you, are more likely to stop too short than reach too far.

So let's say you have a dream that seems completely impossible. Or maybe you had such a dream as a very young person and gave it up as you matured. Perhaps you wanted to be among the world's richest people. And maybe you could have realized that dream, though it's unlikely. Or maybe you wanted to play ball professionally, another unlikely goal for most of us whose talents are more limited than our wishes.

But the dream of having more money may well be reachable, if that's what you really want. And although you may not be able to play ball with the pros, you might be able to play with an amateur team or work in the big leagues in another way.

The reach of a dream is something to consider, but not to be daunted by. Your impossible dream might be a clue to a life interest. You can shift an impossible dream to related, possible ones.

Here is an example of how a grand dream served as a direction finder for me.

Something I have long wanted to do is build an architect-designed home. When I moved in 1991 from Chicago to Minneapolis, I looked into doing that. I found a city lot and talked with an architect whom I knew and whose work I admired. He was willing to work with me and my modest budget, though he warned me that, even with the small house we were talking about, I would have to be disciplined in my choices to keep costs down. His idea for a house to fit that lot was intriguing. Two large trees grew in the front yard, and the architect suggested making the second floor the main floor, so the living room would look into their foliage. I was drawn to his ideas, but after thinking carefully about the project, I decided against it. I was concerned about cost overruns and about focusing on building a house when I was also starting a new job. The risks seemed too high.

Instead of building, I bought a South Minneapolis bungalow almost a century old and well within my budget. The bungalow had a partially finished attic, with a fir floor and two windows. After I had been in the house for a while, I decided to make the attic into a master bedroom suite, including office space and a bathroom. I worked with the architect I knew to design the space. I had a tiny bathroom tucked into an existing closet, three skylights added, the floors refinished, and the walls painted. While the renovation did not fulfill my original, large dream of building a house from scratch, I did enjoy the experience of working with the architect to develop the space and of living in rooms designed and finished especially for me. The renovation was stylish and modern, contrasting nicely with the old charm of the main floor.

If I hadn't recognized my dream of building a house, I might never have sought out the architect to help me with my smaller project. The larger dream was the guide for the smaller, more realistic venture.

Try This: Two Wild Minutes

Two Wild Minutes is a brainstorming exercise you can do with friends or by yourself. Two versions are below. Whichever version you do, let yourself think wildly about what you'd like. You can pare down and get real later.

Two Wild Minutes with Friends

1. Give everyone a pencil and paper, and sit down comfortably in a circle, with your backs to each other. You will be taking turns, so decide who will go first. Let's say it's you. Set the timer for two minutes. As soon as the timer starts, begin calling out every wild dream—everything you wish you could do—that comes to your mind. Your friends will write down everything that you say, taking notes as fast as they can. The more outlandish your dream, the better. Keep going until the timer rings. Then move on to the next person and so on, until everyone has had a turn to be "it," and each of you has notes on the others.

2. Now turn to face each other. Here the note takers read back what they've written. As they go through their lists, they should comment, *in an encouraging way only*, on what they notice. For example:

    - Something that you said reminds one of them of something you have done.
    - Someone will offer the name of a person who's done something similar.
    - Someone will comment that they can see you doing something that you mentioned.
    - Someone will identify common elements among your wild ideas.
    - Someone will suggest a strategy for capturing your wild idea in a smaller way.
    - Someone will encourage you to try out an element of your dream.

    Listen to what each person says, and, when all have finished, comment back to them on their contributions. Answer one or more of these questions:

    What appeals to you about what they said?

    What new ideas did you get?

    What ideas do you now have about what might be possible for you?

What clues do you have about turning an impossible dream into a related possible dream?

What might you try?

Continue with step 2 until every dreamer has heard and responded to the note takers' suggestions.

3. For a final step, decide on three things that you not only could do but will do that will lead you toward your dreams. Let your friends know what they are, and set a time to check in with them on your progress.
4. You might use one of the dreams on your list to complete the exercise in chapter 5 called Get Real (page 53).

Two Wild Minutes on Your Own

1. Settle yourself comfortably, and set a timer for two minutes. Write down as fast as you can every wild dream you can imagine, everything you wish you could do. Go for quantity, not quality: the more outlandish your dream, the better. Keep going until the timer rings. (If you need more space, there are additional pages for writing at the end of this book.)

2. Now take a break. Do a few stretches, take a short walk, or make yourself a cup of tea. After the break, look over what you have written, and answer the following questions:

   Have you done anything at all like something you have written, even in a small way? If so, what?

LESSON 4

What are some elements common to more than one of your ideas?

_____
_____
_____
_____

Do any big ideas suggest smaller, more manageable versions of themselves? If so, which ones?

_____
_____
_____
_____

Whom do you know who has done something similar to anything you have written?

_____
_____
_____
_____

Which idea or part of an idea can you see yourself doing?

_____
_____
_____
_____

If you were to try one element of any of your ideas, what would it be?

_____
_____
_____
_____

3. Now decide on three things that you not only could do but will do that would further a possible dream. Give yourself a deadline, and go for it!

_____
_____
_____
_____
_____

4. Consider using one of the dreams on your list to complete the exercise Get Real at the end of chapter 5 (page 53).

Do Your Homework, Consider Trade-Offs, Then Decide

Exactly what would it take to make your dream come true?
Evaluate trade-offs and risks.
Say no freely.
Choosing thoughtfully is a dreaming skill.

In the spring of 1995, at age fifty-one, I was on holiday in Paris with my mom and my sister, Julie, and I felt frustrated with the meagerness of my high school French. So I concocted the dream of spending a month or so there to improve my language skills. I was working for myself by then and figured that with enough advance planning I could arrange my schedule to free up the time. Now it happens that I had a cousin who lived in Paris, and her parents kept a tiny apartment there for times when they visited their daughter and her family. This aunt and uncle, when they heard about my wish, lent me their apartment for all of April 1996.

The time came, and off I went. I settled into their charming place between the Rue de la Roquette and Place Léon Blum, in the eleventh *arrondissement*. The apartment was on the fifth floor of a classic Parisian building, and every day I rode in its old-fashioned, iron-and-glass elevator that belonged on a movie

set. In the apartment, a black suede sofa, leopard-patterned rug, and antique side chairs and dresser furnished the living room, which looked out onto an iron balcony and the neighborhood rooftops. The ancient bathroom fixtures contrasted sharply with the Plexiglas shower stall and the electric towel-warmer my aunt and uncle had installed. The Murphy bed in the single bedroom could be tucked away behind decorative doors, and a folding table and chairs set up for dining. That room had a balcony, too, big enough for one small chair. The narrow kitchen included a two-burner hot plate, a tiny fridge, a toaster oven, an old-fashioned porcelain sink, and barely room to move.

There were no tourist attractions in the neighborhood, no places to change money, no English spoken. Perfect. My cousin's friend Annie agreed to be my tutor. She came to the apartment twice a week for coffee and conversation, and our talks were the basis for my lessons. Between lessons, I practiced my French in the neighborhood, mainly with shopkeepers: at the bakery; the produce market; the *charcuterie*, where two elderly sisters cooked traditional dishes for customers to take home; and the bistro, where I made friends with the proprietor and a waiter or two.

My French improved, the time went by, and I didn't want to leave Paris. I began to wonder, *How I could stay, or come back, for a longer time? How would I support myself? Where would I live? Would it be possible for me to move to Paris for a year or so?*

I started my homework. Some years previously, I'd met a French businessman, Jean-Pierre, at a conference in the United States. He lived near Paris and worked in the same field as I did, developing and delivering leadership skills programs to businesses. Over lunch toward the end of my stay, we talked about the possibility of my working in France. Jean-Pierre thought it would take me a year to a year and a half to improve my French sufficiently to work in French in our field. He also thought there would be work for me at the end of that time.

If I wanted to live and work in France, I would need to support myself while improving my French. *What would it take to do that, to swing that year to a year and a half?* I asked myself. *I need a place to live and enough money to feed myself and occasionally go to a museum or café. Well, I could work at an interim job, teaching English, for example, or work as a tutor or governess, until I became fluent enough to do my "real" work. Or I could use my savings, take out a second mortgage, or do both, and rent out my house. Or I could sell my house.*

I could see that it would be possible for me to realize this dream, and I did additional research, particularly into teaching English to adults. But I didn't come up with anything I thought would work well for me, and the options I found felt too risky. The trade-offs I would have to make were unacceptable, and I decided against pursuing the dream. After I returned home, I continued to practice French, working with a teacher from the Minneapolis branch of the Alliance Française, a school that fosters French language and culture around the world. And I went again to Paris on vacation.

As it turned out, only six years later and in different circumstances, I lived for ten months in the south of France without having to make the trade-offs I had been unwilling to make earlier. (For that story see Lesson 10, One Good Thing Leads to Another.)

What I Learned: Do My Homework, Consider the Trade-offs, and Then Decide

In Paris, when my month was coming to an end and I began to dream of living there, I did my homework so I could be realistic about what it would take to return for an extended time. I recognized the trade-offs I would have to make to realize that dream, and I ultimately said no. Here is a closer look at the three elements of what I learned.

Homework

Homework is the research you do to get the information you need to understand what it would take to go down the path toward a dream. Homework is the groundwork that guides you toward an informed decision. It's the eye-opener, expanding your knowledge of what your dream will involve: its costs, obstacles, and risks—the trade-offs required for the experience you want. (See also Lesson 3, You Already Have What You Need, for another example of how homework helps you with your dream.)

Homework for my dream of living in Paris included my discussion with my colleague who estimated that I would need a year to a year and a half to improve my French sufficiently. I also talked with a French colleague who worked in

London in English. Her English was better than my French by far, and yet she talked about how difficult, how exhausting it was to spend the whole day listening, explaining ideas, and making fine distinctions in her second language. I spoke with people at several organizations that provided English-language instruction, to see if I could support myself that way, and I looked into housing to estimate what a year to eighteen months would cost.

Trade-Offs

Realizing a dream involves *trade-offs*. Identifying and considering the trade-offs and the risks are important reality checks that help with decision making and are a part of doing homework. When I have a clear picture of exactly what the trade-offs are, I can make my choice.

The homework I did to learn what it would take to spend a year in Paris improving my French showed me that the trade-offs I would have to make were costly. Using my home equity by either selling my house or borrowing against it would jeopardize the financial plans I had for retirement. The uncertainty of finding work, while I was concentrating on language study and later when I sought work in my field, was unnerving. I was in my fifties, and I enjoyed my relatively comfortable life in Minneapolis. Did I want to trade that for the penny-pinching existence I might face in Paris?

And I realized that I was free—and ready—to make an informed decision.

The Freedom to Say No

I recognized that, unlike my red-headed jazz singer dream, living and working in Paris was possible for me. But the trade-offs I'd identified—selling my house or borrowing on it, spending a year abroad with uncertain income, the potential exhaustion of working a job that stretched me to the limit of my language ability—seemed too risky, too costly. That understanding freed me to decide, willingly, against pursuing the dream. And that feeling of freedom, the freedom to say no, was an unexpected benefit.

I had learned that lesson once before. Years ago, I lived in a small town in western Wisconsin, and after some time there, I wanted to move to Minneapolis. My house was for sale for many months in a slow market, and I got discouraged. My friend Karen lived in the city. I talked with her about my discouragement and impatience, and learned that she was considering leaving the city. We talked about trading houses, at least for a limited time. We explored the possibility, imagining what it would be like. After lengthy discussion, we decided not to do it. But there was something about having the option and rejecting it that made it easier to wait for my house to sell. Having the option helped me realize the power I had to make something happen, even though ultimately I didn't use the power.

What You Can Do

Whether you are considering an overly ambitious dream or a more manageable one, do your homework to discover and evaluate the trade-offs—the costs and risks that pursuing your dream will incur. Then, if you ultimately decide against that dream, you are likely to do so willingly, with no sense of defeat. If you decide to go ahead, you'll do so with your eyes open.

Here is a story about someone who weighed considerable risks and went ahead:

My brother-in-law, Eddie, was a Peace Corps volunteer in Afghanistan beginning in 1977, just after he graduated from college. Eddie taught English at the college level there and drank in the language and culture of the country. His tour ended abruptly in 1978, when all Americans were pulled out of Afghanistan after the communist coup and the abduction and execution of the American ambassador, a man Eddie knew.

Back home, Eddie earned master's degrees in political science and international affairs, with a focus on Southeast Asia. He wanted to go back to work overseas, but life intervened. He married, and although he and his wife had agreed to go to Asia, they ended up having a child and buying a home, and Eddie went to work for the state of Texas. Over the years he worked his way up in the state system, promoted to increasingly responsible jobs. By the time he was approaching fifty, he was deputy director of a large government agency and the single dad of a son in his late teens.

Eddie did his work well and was successful, but not satisfied. He hadn't gone overseas in almost twenty years, and he chafed at the very bureaucracy he led. Then, in 2004, a tsunami hit Indonesia.

Eddie had a friend, Aaron, who had been a missionary in Indonesia and wanted to do something about the tsunami's devastation. Eddie took a month's

leave from work, and the two men went to Indonesia. Soon after they arrived, as Eddie says, he knew that this was his life. And Aaron, well-to-do, decided to establish a foundation to fund a rebuilding effort.

Fully aware of the trade-offs he would have to make, Eddie left his job four weeks after returning to Texas, and he moved to Banda Aceh, Indonesia.

People thought he was crazy. He was seven short years away from a full pension with the state of Texas, and he was close to his many siblings and to his son. And he was in a new relationship with a woman who, he says, "dumped me as soon as I left for a month." On the other hand, Eddie's home mortgage was almost paid up, he had no other debt, and his son was about to go off to college. And, he figured, he could always come back to state government to finish the remaining years to full retirement.

Eddie became the point person for the efforts of his friend's foundation, Austin International Rescue Operations, in Banda Aceh. He organized the boat builders and fishermen to rebuild the fishing fleet. He spearheaded business development by establishing sustainable industry practices including clean work spaces, ice on board the boats, immediate fish filleting, and vacuum packaging—better quality controls overall—that leveraged the fishermen's skills and created greater market value for their products. He created a partnership with the Asian Development Bank to establish eight marine livelihood business centers that further enhanced the industry.

After he had been in Indonesia for five years, as the work was entering a new phase—to sustain the safer, sounder business practices he had established—the US government was pushing an effort to bring civilian professional development into Afghanistan. Eddie signed on with the US Agency for International Development (USAID) and shipped out. His first job was to direct military spending for civilian development. Then he moved on to a stabilization program, working with local governments to provide basic services, create social networks, and mitigate conflicts without violence, with all credit, as he says, going to the local governments. After five years there, it was time to move on again.

Eddie has just begun his latest adventure, with the Walter Reed Military Medical Research Foundation. The foundation's purpose is to carry out the President's Emergency Plan for AIDS Research (PEPFAR) in six countries. Eddie is PEPFAR's director of administration and operations in Nigeria, where the organization's focus is HIV/AIDS, malaria, and Ebola research, prevention, treatment, and care.

Once Eddie made the decision to leave state government and go to Indonesia, he never looked back. He says he could still return to his old employer, but he doubts he will. He followed—is still following—his dream of working overseas. His interest in other languages and cultures continues unabated, as does his excitement about the work and the opportunities to contribute. Eddie was and is realistic about his trade-offs, but for him the dream is well worth making them. As he approaches sixty, he has as much enthusiasm for his new adventure as he had for his first one as a Peace Corps volunteer over thirty-five years ago.

Try This: Get Real

Answer these questions:

1. What is your most ambitious dream—not completely outlandish, perhaps, but a far reach?

   _____
   _____
   _____

2. What about that dream most appeals to you? For example, a main reason for my wanting to spend a year in Paris was to become fluent in French. I am thrilled when I can carry on a conversation in French and I realize I'm not translating but thinking in my second language. That's what I wanted to accomplish in Paris. Think about your dream, and answer the question, Why do you want it?

   _____
   _____
   _____
   _____
   _____

3. What would it take to make your dream come true? What are the costs and risks involved? Consider:

Time

Money

Family and relationships

Work

Information

Skills and tools

_____
_____
_____

Geography or other circumstances

_____
_____
_____

Other issues

_____
_____
_____

4. About which of the above issues do you need to learn more, and which of the following resources might help you with that? Note which resources might help with which issue:

_____
_____
_____

Friends and family members

_____
_____
_____

56 Business acquaintances

_____
_____
_____

Online resources

_____
_____
_____

Books, maps, or other material

_____
_____
_____

Statistical, budget, or income information

_____
_____
_____

5. Which element or elements of your dream could you begin to learn more about, or begin doing right away, even if your beginning is small?

_____
_____
_____

6. And finally, write down three things you will do to begin to follow your dream and when you will do them.

   What will you do?   **When or by when?**

   1. _____   _____

   2. _____   _____

   3. _____   _____

Now Consider This: Choosing Thoughtfully Is a Dreaming Skill

Realizing a dream often requires weighing and then choosing between two present, conflicting desires, or between short-term and long-term wants. Only the person involved can perform the balancing act necessary to solve these dilemmas. Solving them—making choices—is, for most of us, a skill necessary for dreaming.

Here are two examples, each presenting a slightly different dilemma.

Six Silver Spoons

When Mom and Dad were married, someone gave them, as a wedding gift, six silver spoons. The year was 1938, the Depression was underway, and the newlyweds were strapped for money. They made a practical decision and traded the spoons for a set of pots and pans.

Years later, when I was well into adulthood, Mom told me that she regretted that decision. She said she should have kept the spoons. If she had, she said, she and my dad would certainly have gotten the pots and pans they needed

some other way. Then, over the years, Mom would have managed to add a piece of silver flatware here and a piece there, and eventually she would have had a set. As it was, with the births and raising of three children and the purchase of a home, my parents never had money for that kind of luxury. Until shortly before her death at ninety-seven, Mom continued to invite guests to her apartment for meals, and she would have loved to set her table with silver.

Mom regretted the practical decision she had made years ago, because that decision made it more difficult for her to begin and expand a collection of sterling silver tableware. She regretted that the short-term need had taken precedence over the longer-term pleasure.

Sarah in Paris

My friend Sarah visited me in Paris during the April I spent there. Our circumstances were remarkably similar: she and I did the same work, had roughly the same income, were both single moms of young adult children, and were both homeowners. At the time, I was building a cabin during the summers (see Lesson 7, Start Without Knowing the End), completing it gradually as I had time and money to do so. Sarah talked with me about that project; she didn't see how I could afford it.

During the course of her stay, she and I went shopping for gifts to take back for family and friends. Sarah, always generous, bought expensive gifts—designer silk scarves, perfumes from Parisian *parfumeurs*, and the like. I, ever watchful, bought soaps and little boxes of chocolates from specialty shops, and coasters and small prints from the stalls of the *bouquinistes* on the Left Bank. Sarah clearly took pleasure in choosing gifts for the people in her life, but the difference in our expenditures was marked, and the money I didn't spend on gifts went into the cabin.

I love bringing souvenirs of my travels home for friends, and I choose them with pleasure. Friends know I'm thinking about them, but I'm careful, because I have other dreams.

We all constantly confront competing demands for our time, money, energy, and attention, and we have both short-term and long-term considerations about how to spend those resources. What is convenient and even realistic right now may make a future dream more difficult to reach. What is more expensive now may make a future dream impossible.

No one but you can weigh your short-term and long-term desires. Often, though, you may need to endure some belt-tightening now if you want to reach a larger dream next month, next year, or five years from now.

What You Can Do

Many of us have multiple goals, some short-term, some long-term. And most of us do not have the time, energy, patience, or money to satisfy them all. Identifying—noticing—what we most want and being willing to set priorities can help us make our trade-offs.

We can talk with a friend about what we want. We can listen to ourselves as we speak and to what our friend says in response. This simple talking and listening can sharpen our understanding of what is most important. Or we can weigh the alternatives ourselves.

Try This: Weigh It

The purpose of this exercise is to help you think through the dilemma created by conflicting desires. In the first part, you'll consider a past experience; in the second, a current dilemma.

A Past Experience

Think of a time in the past when you couldn't decide between two things you wanted. For example, you wanted season tickets to the local baseball team's home games you always shared with friends. On the other hand, your living room sofa and favorite chair were getting threadbare, and you wanted to replace them. But you couldn't do both. Or you wanted something right then, say a weekend in Chicago, and something bigger later, maybe a vacation in Europe.

What were your conflicting desires?

_____

_____

_____

How did you weigh the alternatives? What were the pros and cons of each?

_____
_____
_____
_____
_____

What did you do? What compromises, if any, did you make?

_____
_____
_____
_____
_____

How did you feel as a result? What did you learn?

_____
_____
_____
_____
_____

A Current Dilemma

Now think of a current dilemma involving two conflicting wants or a long-term versus a short-term want. Record the two sides of the dilemma on lines A and B under the balance scale.

Then list the pros and cons, advantages and disadvantages, of each side of the dilemma on the charts below.

A: _____   **B:** _____

Side A	
Pros	Cons

Side B	
Pros	Cons

What insights do you have now about your dilemma?

_____
_____
_____
_____

DO YOUR HOMEWORK, CONSIDER TRADE-OFFS, THEN DECIDE

I can't advise you how to choose, except to say that when I slow down and am quiet, when I listen to myself, when I consider advantages and disadvantages, the answer becomes clear to me. The more relaxed I am, the less I am swayed by the insistent voice that speaks to me when I feel impatient or when I'm envious of things other people have or do. The quieter I am, the more I listen to myself, the more in touch I am with myself, the easier it is to set priorities and choose between conflicting desires.

Address Obstacles and Focus on Elements

How do you stand in your own way?
How do others limit you?
What are the elements of your dream?

When my son was very young, our family spent vacation time canoeing, mainly on Wisconsin rivers. I enjoyed those canoe trips. I loved being outside, on the water, carrying everything we needed. Yet every time we came to small rapids, even a riffle in the stream, I got nervous. I noticed that my worry in anticipation of rapid water was diminishing my pleasure in canoeing. Although I wasn't interested in whitewater canoeing in general—far from it—I didn't want to miss the mainly calm rivers we chose just because of a few riffles, and I didn't want to feel afraid of them. I wanted to enjoy our canoe trips, from the planning to the drive home.

The Sierra Club offered a whitewater canoe clinic on the Peshtigo and Pike Rivers in eastern Wisconsin over a summer weekend. I gathered my courage and decided to take it. I hoped it would help me navigate the water currents better and overcome my fear of small rapids.

Feeling nervous, I left my husband and small son at home and drove to the meeting place by myself. I was paired with another single paddler, a woman I didn't know. Twelve of us took the course. We worked with our instructors, Ted and Joan, a husband and wife team, first in a classroom and then on the water. They were intrepid, and I remember clearly Joan's saying that she would "paddle into hell with Ted." I knew I would never feel that way, and yet as we moved from navigating calm water to slight riffles, I learned to read the water and take advantage of its current, rather than fighting the current as I had been doing. For the first time, I enjoyed canoeing through the riffles. We gradually practiced on more rapid water, and although my nervousness grew with each increase in water speed (and noise), I paddled through with my partner without difficulty. My anxiety took a big jump when we came to the final rapids—tumbling, noisy water that I couldn't imagine going through and didn't want to go through. But together, as we had done all along, the whole group, with our instructors, scouted the rapids from upstream, planning the best route. We took our time, until every paddler knew exactly what to do. Then, one canoe at a time, we went through. I was scared, but when our turn came, my partner and I negotiated those rapids flawlessly.

I was happy we had come through the rapids so well and glad I had done the weekend clinic. Although I still was not interested in whitewater canoeing in general, the course helped me manage the smaller rapids that are part of so many rivers. I looked forward to and enjoyed our family's canoe trips much more than I had before the clinic. I felt less nervous, more competent and confident. I had gotten out of my own way, managing my fears, and I was proud of myself.

My fear of rapid water was an internal obstacle. Often, the obstacles to our pursuing a dream are external—a partner who doesn't share the dream, for example. Other reasons are lack of money, lack of time, responsibility for children, friends or relatives who might not approve, work, a busy schedule. We and others accept these reasons automatically and may not consider that within the relationship, the budget, and the schedule there might be ways to realize at least part of the dream, elements of what we'd love.

In the following example, my uncle was able to realize elements of his dream, even though his wife, my aunt, didn't share the dream at all.

Uncle Jerome, my father's youngest brother, loved the water. He was in the navy during World War II, and for the rest of his life he was fascinated with boats. An engineer by profession, he was a fine craftsman, and he worked meticulously, building cabinets and other home projects. Naturally, he became a boat builder in his spare time.

Uncle Jerome built two kayaks and then a more ambitious boat, a fourteen-foot Rangeley. The Rangeley is an oar boat derived from an 1860 design meant for the Rangeley Lakes in Maine, shallow lakes with frequent high waters and strong winds. He named the Rangeley for my aunt, *Bernice K.*

Uncle Jerome and Aunt Bernice had two children, a dog, two children-in-law, three grandchildren, and several grand-dogs in common. They shared a dry sense of humor and a great love of travel, and they had been married for fifty-eight years when Uncle Jerome died in 2010. All that time, Aunt Bernice wanted nothing to do with boats or water. She was afraid of the water; when they visited me in northern Wisconsin in the mid-'90s, Jerome and I went sailing on Lake Superior on my little boat, and Aunt Bernice stayed on the deck of their B&B, overlooking the water and happily reading.

When Uncle Jerome launched the *Bernice K* in May 1977 on the Schuylkill River in Philadelphia, Aunt Bernice threw a launching party for him on the riverbank, but she never left the shore.

Perhaps if Aunt Bernice had shared Uncle Jerome's love of boats, they would have spent vacation time on the water, owned a larger boat, even lived on a boat. But she didn't, and Uncle Jerome found ways to realize his love of boats and the sea on his own, sharing other interests with Aunt Bernice.

What I Learned: Address Obstacles and Focus on Elements

Sometimes the limitations we call "reasons" become excuses for not doing anything. My internal obstacle, the fear of rapid water, might have stopped me from taking the canoe clinic that made all subsequent canoe trips a pleasure. The prize—enjoyable canoe trips, both in the anticipation and in the doing—was worth braving my fears for. Among other things, I learned that I could be nervous and still act. That's not to say I would take on any physical challenge, or push myself through any fear. I am not physically courageous and am not interested, for example, in technical mountain climbing, deep sea diving, parachute jumping, or whitewater raft guiding. And I certainly can't

say for you or anyone else what challenge is worth braving a fear for. Only you can do that for yourself. But for my love of canoeing and the pleasure I took in family canoe trips, it was well worth pushing through my nervousness and completing the whitewater canoe clinic.

In the case of Uncle Jerome, the external obstacle of his wife's not sharing his dream led him to identify elements that he could realize and Aunt Bernice could support. He knew that, although he would prefer to share fully his love of boats and the water with her, he didn't have to settle for nothing. He was able to capture some of the elements of his dream: building and launching several boats, one of which he named for her.

What You Can Do

You, too, can recognize and address internal and external obstacles to your dream. You can ask yourself:

How am I getting in my own way, and how can I step aside?

What would it take for me to overcome my own resistance to be able to do something I long to do?

What are the external factors that limit me? Consider:

- a partner's reluctance or disapproval
- what others might think
- time
- money

What are the elements of my dream, and how can I begin to realize them?

You can focus on the elements of your dream that appeal to you, with a view toward incorporating some of those elements into your life right now.

I've noticed that when I consider the elements of something I'd love to do, the understanding that I might realize some of those elements diminishes the obstacles I've identified.

Making a start—pursuing elements of a dream as opposed to the whole dream—reduces the obstacles because pursuing elements requires less time, money, effort, and intrusion on others' wishes than does taking on a larger dream. And smaller beginnings often lead to bigger possibilities.

For example, for years I had the dream of living on a sailboat. And, for years, that seemed impossible: the obstacles were legion, and I assumed such a dream was for others. But when I thought about why I wanted to live on a sailboat, I was able to identify elements of that big dream, which included:

- living an outdoor life
- being on the water
- knowing how to sail a boat myself
- becoming more self-sufficient
- meeting new people
- speaking another language
- travelling to new places to see both famous and everyday sites

I deliberately incorporated those elements into my life in other satisfying ways, short of my all-encompassing dream.

While I pursued elements of my dream, like taking sailing lessons and joining a French conversation group, I did not feel as if I were settling for second best. I did what I could with the resources I had. All the while, I met people with similar interests who gave me new ideas. I became aware of more opportunities. Starting small expanded my experience and my thinking. And eventually, I realized my big dream (see Lesson 10, One Good Thing Leads to Another).

In a most poignant story of addressing obstacles and focusing on elements, my high school friend Carolyn made an astounding and complex trade-off as her fortieth birthday drew near.

Carolyn had fallen in love with David in college. They had tried but could not make a go of their relationship, and later both married other people. Carolyn's marriage was brief and childless, and after her marriage ended, she met Barry, and they got together. Barry did not want to marry or have children, as Carolyn dreamed of doing, but they were a couple until Carolyn was in her late thirties. By that time, as she said, she was struggling to figure out what to do, "given that our dreams were very different." David, in the meantime, had had two children, and when they were school-aged, he and his wife divorced.

During the time when Carolyn was having doubts about staying with Barry, she and David started to see each other. When they were doing so, "with some intent," as Carolyn put it, she moved out of the place she shared with Barry to live with a friend for a while. Barry, understanding that he might really lose Carolyn, changed his mind, besieged her with his regrets, and said, "Yes, I do want to get married and have children. It took this for me to know that."

Carolyn chose to continue to see David, the man she later told me she realized she had always loved. As they grew closer, David made it clear that, although he wasn't ruling it out, he was unwilling to commit to having another child. He liked his job as a modestly paid Legal Aid attorney, and a good chunk of his income went for child support. Also, he wanted Carolyn to make the decision to be with him without a guarantee that he would be open to their having a baby. Carolyn felt the tug of Barry's change of heart, now that he was offering what she had wanted for so long, and of her own yearning to be with David.

Ultimately, when Carolyn was thirty-eight and David forty-one, Carolyn chose David. They moved in together in November and were married the following May.

In August of the same year, while they were attending a friend's wedding, Carolyn said, "I suddenly realized through some subtle shift that David had said yes to himself to our trying to get pregnant. When I asked, he agreed that yes, he had shifted."

So at forty, as Carolyn says, she was "pregnant and happy as a clam." The following May, Gabriel was born, and six years later, Micah, their bonus baby, joined the family.

Carolyn and David are now seventy-one and seventy-four. Their boys are young adults and on their own. David is retired; Carolyn, a counselor, works part time; and they are settled in their lives in eastern Pennsylvania. Recently they discovered English country dancing—Carolyn has been a folk dancer since high school—and she and David go dancing twice a week.

Try This: Tree of Elements

1. Identify a dream, and write the name of the dream on the trunk of the tree.
2. Think of as many elements—as many pieces and parts of that dream—as you can, and write each element on one of the tree's leaves. Include any part of your dream that appeals to you, big or small, exotic or mundane.

3. Using your completed tree, consider the following, and write your thoughts in the spaces below:

Which of these elements appeal to you most?

_____
_____
_____
_____

Which elements do you already experience?

Which elements would you like to have more of?

What can you do to incorporate more of what you'd like?

_____
_____
_____
_____
_____
_____
_____

Start Without Knowing the End

There is power in not knowing.
Don't wait. Begin!

From 1984 through 1992, I spent a week each summer on the south shore of Lake Superior at my friends' cabin. The cabin, an A-frame facing the lake, was on a spit of land that stretched partway across the bottom of Bark Bay, near Cornucopia, Wisconsin, and I had to paddle across a slough to get there. My friends would leave a canoe for me at the little parking lot across the slough. I loved the place, and I wished from my first visit that I could have my own cabin. But that seemed way out of reach—impossible.

In early 1992, with my son graduated from college and launched, I left my job at the consulting firm, struck out on my own as a freelancer, and got a puppy. He was a black standard poodle, and I named him Cole Porter after my favorite songwriter. When I took Cole up to the cabin that summer, he was ecstatic—the freedom, the smells, the water, the beach, the scruffy woods growing out of sandy soil on the narrow strip of land. Watching Cole, I thought,

He looks the way I feel, and at that moment I decided to find a small piece of land of my own, land I could reach by car.

My freelance business was just a few months old, and I had no idea if it would be successful. I arranged for an equity line of credit on my house, figuring I could sell a Lake Superior property if my business didn't go well. Land is sold on the south shore not by the acre but by the number of feet of shoreline, with 150 feet the least the zoning laws allowed. I bought 160 feet, high on a cliff—a wedge of two acres of land. I couldn't get down to the water, but beachfront was way more expensive, and I had a knockout view of the lake. And there was a beach a short walk up the gravel road. My land was wooded with maple, birch, evergreens, a few mountain ash, and one tall, young, healthy oak tree. Thimbleberry bushes and big ferns grew in the shady understory. I closed on the land late in the fall of 1992.

Jeff, the neighbor from whom I'd bought the parcel, had sold part of his property and kept the piece next to mine, where he had built his cabin. He had used a sauna kit to build a tiny log cabin, adding an even smaller shed and a little log outhouse with a window facing the lake. The following summer, 1993, I set up a big canvas tent on my land. Jeff suggested I use his driveway and outhouse. Cole and I beat a short path from Jeff's driveway through the woods to our tent, and Jeff put up a sign on the path: *Abby's Road*. I put a cot, a little rug, a bed for Cole, and a low table in the tent, and set up a picnic table outside. I brought up a camp stove, a cooler, and collapsible water containers. I got water at an artesian spring at the public beach two miles down the highway, stored my food in the trunk of the car, and I was in business. Whenever I didn't have work—most of the time at that point—Cole and I headed north. I hoped that someday I might build something more substantial than the tent, but that dream would not be realized in the foreseeable future. Or so I thought.

At that time, two of my neighbors in Minneapolis, Bill and Jerry, were also in job transitions. We would meet for coffee two or three mornings a week to solve the problems of the world, not to mention encourage each other, before hitting the pavement to look for work. One morning in the summer of 1993, we were talking about my land purchase and how I had my own camping spot on the lake. Bill, a carpenter, said he'd always wanted to build a small cabin, and if I'd buy the materials, he'd build. Jerry, a real estate developer, said he was in. Suddenly, my dream was a lot closer than I could have imagined.

I roughed out a plan on graph paper for a 15-foot-by-12-foot cabin (180 square feet), a glorified wooden tent with a storage loft. I pictured the cabin as a step up from the canvas tent I was using. But I talked about the project with my architect friend, John, who suggested a larger footprint. He said that over time I would appreciate the additional space. He suggested enlarging the cabin to 20 feet by 20 feet for the best use—least waste—of the 4-by-8-foot plywood sheets that would form the walls, floor, and roof of the building. I redrew the plan for a 400-square-foot cabin with a sleeping loft.

On summer weekends and into early fall that year, and for part of the summer of 1994, Bill, Jerry, and I built the cabin shell. We had a lot of unexpected help. The owner of the local lumberyard, Donnie, took an interest in the project. He had a fine sense of how much we'd get done each weekend, and he delivered just the right materials to the site before we got there. He said he didn't want lumber and other stuff sitting outside in the weather. He gave us tips on windows and doors we could salvage, found an old library ladder for me for the loft, and sent me to see other cabins under construction in the area to get ideas. He lent us equipment, including a power saw once when Bill left his at home.

Friends would ask if they could work with us, and I would say, "Let me check the schedule." Somehow there was always room for additional help. Together, we finished the foundation, the subfloor, and the walls, including plastic-covered insulation. We put in the doors and windows and got the roof on, hiring help after Jerry almost fell off. We installed the floor joists for the loft and roughed out the kitchen counter and interior bathroom walls. A realtor friend told me about a used wood-burning stove for sale in a house she was listing. I bought it, and we installed it. A high school shop student designed the wiring as a school project, and his teacher, a friend of mine, wired the cabin. Bill and Jerry and I put in the composting toilet; I didn't have a well dug and didn't have running water in the cabin, choosing instead to get my water at the artesian spring. (Some years later, I had a well and real plumbing installed.)

During the time we were building, I kept in touch with John, the architect, and he continued to make suggestions. They included deeper floor insulation and 6-inch studs instead of 4-inch to accommodate thicker insulation in the walls. He also suggested placing the wood stove in the middle of the room, where it would serve as the literal and figurative heart of the cabin.

John told me that the main mistake people make in building cabins is not putting in enough windows to take advantage of the view, because windows are

expensive. He designed a wall of windows facing the lake. At his suggestion, I used ready-cut patio door glass from a discount place for the center windows—I was surprised at their low cost—and splurged on full-view doors at each end for air, additional light, and an expanded lake view. I had glass cut to size and tempered for the windows in the gable. The result was dramatic and beautiful—the whole wall is glass.

By mid-summer 1994, the cabin was usable, if not entirely lovely, and I took down the tent and moved in. The larger, more comfortable cabin took longer to build than a smaller version would have but was well worth the additional time, effort, patience, and money. And all in all, the whole process was relaxed.

Building the cabin was much more work than we had anticipated, and Bill had a new girlfriend who wanted his company on weekends. For those and other reasons, we stopped building toward the end of the summer of 1994. By that time, my business was perking along, and I was able to finish paying down my home equity loan and begin hiring local craftspeople to continue the cabin work. I didn't want to go into debt, so for the next six summers I hired skilled work done as I could afford it, continued to do some of the work myself and with friends, and enjoyed my place in its various stages all the while. By the summer of 2000, the cabin was about done: cedar siding and shakes on the outside; interior side walls, cathedral ceiling, and floor finished in pine; back and front walls dry-walled and painted red; kitchen shelves full of dishes, pots, books. An apartment-sized stove and under-the-counter fridge, a table salvaged from the trash and refinished, a pullout sofa, the floor in the sleeping loft, a futon bed. In total, the cabin had taken eight summers to finish.

The whole process had unexpected benefits and satisfactions. One example: after I paid back the equity line of credit, I didn't go into debt again. At times, when I was busy with work, I was tempted to take out a loan to just get the cabin done. But working for myself meant that sometimes I had more work, sometimes less, and I stuck with my decision not to incur debt. I was glad of that, and proud of myself. Time went by, the cabin was finished, and I was debt-free.

Another example was less tangible: one of the carpenters, Kent, came along fairly late in the building. He did a fine job on the front deck, the interior pine paneling, and the hold-everything shelves on the back wall of the kitchen. Kent, who was from Minneapolis, had his own dream of finding enough work up north to allow him to buy a piece of land up there and build a cabin for himself. The good work he did for me was a beginning, and I felt happy about my contribution to his dream.

What I Learned: There Is Power in Not Knowing

Conventional wisdom advises us to set a goal and work to accomplish it. We learn that reaching the goal requires concentration, sacrifice, and a dogged insistence on getting the end result. I suggest another approach. Even if we can't map out all the steps needed to realize a dream, we can take the first step toward what we'd love, a step that's possible now. Then we can look for an opportunity to take a next step, and then a next. As we continue, other ideas will occur to us, and new opportunities will present themselves. We can adjust as we go. We don't have to tense up, to grit our teeth. We can take one step at a time without precisely knowing what the next one will be.

I took a first step—bought the land—without knowing if or when I could manage to build a cabin. I was happy in the tent. Being willing to not know gave me a kind of power. I didn't have a rigid plan, and there was no way I could fail. I could, and did, concentrate on the process—enjoying camping on my own land with some practical help from my neighbor—and, as unexpected opportunities came up, I wended my way toward my dream.

The outcome, all these years after completion, still amazes me. The cabin is beautiful inside and out. The exterior cedar siding and shakes, finished with bleaching oil, have weathered to a light grey. The varnished interior pine paneling has darkened to a warm honey color, and the soft red front and back walls provide a welcome contrast to the wood, and look beautiful whether framing the view of summer leaves or winter snow. The furniture, though a little beat up, is colorful and comfortable. Mementos decorate the walls, rugs cover the pine floor, and books fill the shelves. When the temperature drops, the small cast-iron stove in the middle of the room heats the cabin in no time. From the loft bedroom, I can gaze through the gable windows at the woods out back or the lake in front. The windows on all sides of the cliff-top cabin catch cooling summer breezes that discourage insects. The sunny deck at the back and the shaded one in front are comfortable for

many months each year. I can't see my neighbors from my place, and I can still shower in the summer on the back deck under a plastic sun shower, in water that's heated naturally. Everything works, and the cabin is even better than my dreams.

What You Can Do

I suggest you embrace the idea that you can begin without having everything you need in place, and without knowing exactly how it will all work out. In other words, *don't wait!*

Here is an example of someone who took an early, phased retirement so she could get started on her dream sooner—a start that led her to an undreamed-of adventure.

Maria, a Chinese American friend, was a professor of dance at the University of Minnesota and active as a dancer, actor, and playwright in the Minneapolis and St. Paul dance and theater communities, including with the Asian-centric Theater Mu (now Mu Performing Arts). Yet from her large, gracious condo near downtown St. Paul, Maria dreamed of living a more quiet life in the mountains. When she began her phased early retirement from the university in 2000, Maria sold her condo and bought a place outside of Denver, at 9,600 feet, with a grand view of the Rockies. For five years she came back to Minnesota for one semester each year, bunking with a friend, to fulfill her reduced teaching requirements. During the rest of the year she lived more quietly in Colorado. When she was fully retired in 2006, she moved there permanently.

Maria's planned quiet life after retirement was not so quiet. She became active in local community theater in Denver, as she had done in Minneapolis. When she was cast in a production of *The Joy Luck Club*, she met Tria, a fellow Asian American actor also in the play. As they got to know each other, they talked about how there were few parts in local theater for Asian American actors and no theater that focused on Asian Americans and their lives. One late night, as Maria tells it, she and Tria were relaxing "over one or two too many glasses of wine." One of them asked, "How come there isn't an Asian American theater company here?" The other answered, "I dunno. Wanna start one?" And again as Maria says, "like all wine-induced great ideas, TEA—Theater Esprit Asia—was born. Just like that."

Maria is as efficient and businesslike as she is creatively talented, and she and Tria offered their friends and colleagues a chance to invest, however modestly, in their idea. The response was overwhelming, and in 2013 TEA premiered to fine reviews and enthusiastic audiences. By the end of its first season, TEA had garnered four coveted awards, was financially stable, and was led by a strong, able, and active board of directors.

Maria had no idea when she followed her original dream of living a quiet life in the mountains what it would lead to after she "retired." When Maria took that first step and began living year-round in Colorado, an unexpected opportunity appeared. Her dream expanded, and she took another step and another, culminating in a creative success—in the seventh decade of her life—that she could not have imagined at the start.

Try This: Three Dreams

Find a quiet moment when you can sit down and relax. Clear your mind. Close your eyes, take a deep breath, and imagine a favorite spot.

Now think of at least three things you would really love, three things you wish for. Perhaps you'd like to start a cake-baking business, volunteer to help the homeless, make time to exercise each day, or keep a diary. Perhaps you'd like to see Yellowstone National Park or visit your best friend from high school. Perhaps you'd like to change jobs. Maybe you're not sure what you'd like. Don't push your mind to invent these dreams. Rather, take your time and let your thinking flow. Then, when ideas occur to you, write three of them down. You might start by using the spaces on the next few pages.

For each dream, write a first step you could take to begin. For a cake-baking business, you might make your favorite cake and give a piece to each of several friends. To begin volunteer work, you might visit a homeless shelter or talk with someone who is already working at one. To exercise or keep a diary regularly, you might take a walk today, or get a notebook and make the first entry, even if you can't envision doing it every day.

Now add two more steps for each dream, so that you have on paper the first three things you could do to begin making each dream come true. In the cake-baking example, you might ask these friends to be your board of directors, helping you select other recipes and acting as your official tasters.

Lesson 7

Dream 1

Step 1

Step 2

Step 3

Dream 2

Step 1

Step 2

Step 3

Dream 3

Step 1

Step 2

_____
_____
_____

Now pick just one of your three dreams, and note *when* you could take the very first step for that dream. And when that time comes, take the step.

I will begin this dream:

_____

_____

And I will take the first step on or by this date:

_____

Relationships Pave the Way for Luck

Your community is an essential resource and includes
people who are close to you and some who are not.
Every interaction is an opportunity.

In the spring of 1991, after I'd been working at my dream job for three years, my company moved me from its regional office in Chicago to company headquarters in Minneapolis. In preparation for the move, I put my condo in Chicago up for sale and, after exploring and rejecting my dream of building a house, began looking for a home in Minneapolis.

I worked with Ilsa, a realtor who showed me many homes. We found a house I liked near Lake Harriet, a bungalow in a neighborhood of mostly larger homes. The first time Ilsa and I saw the house, the owners were away. When I wanted to see it a second time before making an offer, they were at home. They sat in the backyard while Ilsa and I went through the house again. Afterwards, and although Ilsa said it usually wasn't done, I went outside to meet them.

On that late spring day, the homeowners and I sat in the sun and chatted. They were empty-nesters, she a retired librarian and he a still-active pastor.

They were moving to southern Minnesota, where he would have a new church, and they were planning to downsize and travel more now that their daughter was a young adult. They asked me about myself and learned that I had lived near Minneapolis before and was happy to be returning to the area. I, too, had a child who would shortly graduate from college and was planning to move to Minneapolis. We talked pleasantly in that way for fifteen minutes or so, and then Ilsa and I were on our way.

Ilsa knew that these people had turned down a previous offer for their house, and she knew what the offer had been. I was able to make a higher bid and stay within my budget, but my offer was contingent on selling my Chicago condo before closing on the Minneapolis house. I couldn't afford two mortgages, and the market at the time was slow. I didn't know how long it would take to sell my place. I understood that if another acceptable offer on the Minneapolis house came in, I would have to either remove the contingency or let the house go.

Sure enough, a few weeks later the couple had another offer. By that time, I was picturing myself in the house and in the neighborhood, delighted at the prospect of living there, and even though my condo hadn't sold, I decided to remove the contingency. The house would be mine, and I was thrilled.

After the Minneapolis closing, Ilsa told me that the last bid on the house came from the same couple whose previous offer had been turned down, and that their new offer was about 3 percent higher than mine. According to the fine print in my contingency-offer document, and something I hadn't realized, the homeowners could have accepted the higher offer even though I removed the contingency. The owners said, however, that they could see me in the house and they liked the idea of my living there. They decided to accept my slightly lower offer once I removed the contingency. I was nervous about doing that because my Chicago condo hadn't sold, but I thought I could tighten my belt and manage two payments for a few months if necessary. And as it turned out, I carried two mortgages for just one month before the condo sold.

Friends said I was lucky to get the house. I was. And I think if I hadn't had that backyard conversation with the owners, they would have accepted the higher offer, and I would have lost the house. I didn't go out to the backyard with my own advantage in mind. I was just curious about the people who lived in the house I liked so much, and took the opportunity to meet them. Our conversation was not a strategy on my part, but it created a relationship that, ephemeral though it was, paved the way for my good luck.

Over the eleven years I lived there, the house became my dream home, and I loved it more and more as time went by. I sold it only to help make a larger dream—my sailing adventure with Tom (see Lesson 10, One Good Thing Leads to Another)—come true.

What I Learned: My Community Is an Essential Resource

Over and over again, I have learned this lesson—that my community is a great and essential resource, not the least for helping me realize my dreams. I have relied on family, friends, and acquaintances throughout my life. They have been interested and generous, and I hope I have been so in return. I have gained emotional and spiritual support, ideas and wisdom from them and sometimes from strangers. I have also gotten tangible help, including problem solving, planning or assistance completing a project, tools, even the loan of an apartment. Thinking of example after example, I am so touched. I feel fortunate and rich.

What You Can Do

Most interactions with others include two components. One is the business at hand, and the other is the relationship between you and the other person. Each meeting or conversation is an opportunity not only to accomplish the task but to enhance, maintain, or detract from that relationship. With family members, for example, the task might be to plan a vacation: Where will we go? How will we get there? What will we do? The planning process itself reflects the relationship component. Does everyone have a chance to contribute? Does one person shoot down another person's idea? Do family members appreciate a range of suggestions?

Even on mundane errands, these components emerge. When I go to the shoemaker, the business may be to pick up mended shoes. The relationship

aspect encompasses whatever happens between me and the shoemaker. Do we have a pleasant exchange? Do I express satisfaction with his work? Or if I'm not satisfied, what is the tone of my complaint? Does my behavior strengthen or diminish the relationship?

You can cultivate awareness of the importance of your circle of relationships. The circle includes people you know and see on a regular basis, and those who are more distant. Even when people step into your circle briefly, as did the owners of the house I bought in Minneapolis, consider carefully how you wish to use that opportunity. More often, though, it's the longer-term relationships that help pave our way. Here is an example from my friend Luann, told in her own words.

> For ten years I directed a small nonprofit that advocates for poor children. We welcomed interns to further the reach of our four-person staff.
>
> One fall, Steve, an undergrad at the University of Minnesota, walked in and asked if he could volunteer so he could learn a little about what we did and how we did it. Of course, we said yes.
>
> He proved to be so wonderful that we were able to hire him to do a project the summer before his senior year, during which he was debating whether to become a pediatrician or an educator to further his work on behalf of children.
>
> Steve was the first undergrad in the history of the University of Minnesota to deliver the commencement address, which he did just before departing for Harvard Medical School.
>
> After that, I lost track of him, though every year or two I would wonder what he was up to and how in the world I could find him.
>
> About twelve years later, there was a knock on my front door in the spring. Who was standing there, with a petition to allow a new garage to be built two houses away? Steve! He and his wife and young family were being moved to Minneapolis on a Center for Disease Control fellowship and had two days to buy a house before flying back to their home in Atlanta.

I became the extra grandma to their growing family, and was THRILLED when they asked me if they could take me along to Cambodia while they volunteered at one of the country's two children's hospitals and scoped out the schools for possible relocation. Talk about luck! I love to travel, but I would never have experienced Cambodia if I had not said yes to an undergrad volunteer who cared about kids.

Here's a shorter, more immediate example. I have a friend, a fellow sailor from Switzerland. Dan was a long-distance truck driver in Europe when he was a young man, before he moved to the States. His best friend at the time was a dispatcher who worked for the same trucking company. Dan told me that during the winters, his friend made sure to route him through southern Italy, France, Spain, and Portugal. During the summers his friend routed Dan up north! And that's how their relationship paved the way for Dan's luck.

Try This: Community Circles

The circle has long been a metaphor for community. When I was a girl, my mom belonged to a sewing circle, and those neighborhood women formed a community. As a youngster and as a teenager, I had my own circle of friends that excluded my parents and siblings. As adults, we have our circles of friends, our political circles, our professional circles, our religious circles. In our daily lives, we often include and help people in our circles, and they include and help us. We may not be as generous to people outside of our circles, or think of them as often, and we may not accept them as readily. For centuries, for example, parents have come between lovers who are not of the same circles. I suggest that people in our circles are essential to our dreaming and making dreams come true. The wider our circles are, the more potential we have to get help and to give it.

The circles in the illustration on page 89 represent your community. Follow the directions on page 88 to explore your relationships with the people in your community.

1. In the center of the concentric circles, write your name or draw a small figure that represents you. In the next circle nearest the center, write the names of the people closest to you. In the third circle, add names of the next tier of friends and family, and in the fourth, names in your fourth tier. You don't have to include everyone you know, but add a representative sample.
2. For each name on each tier, note one way that person has helped you. Perhaps the person has done something as simple as picking up an item from the store for you, or as complicated as helping you build a tool shed, or as important as providing child care. The idea is to think about how people in your community have enriched your life.
3. Now, outside the circles, add remote acquaintances or even strangers, perhaps a woman on the bus or a man selling flowers at the farmers' market. Note how each of those people helped you, perhaps with an idea or a sympathetic ear.
4. Reflect a second time on each person on your chart, this time considering how you have helped them.
5. Extra credit: Look at the names on your list. Is there someone whom you would like to move from an outer circle to an inner one? How could you make that happen?
6. What insights and ahas do you have now about the people in your community? Record your ideas on the lines below.

_____
_____
_____
_____
_____
_____

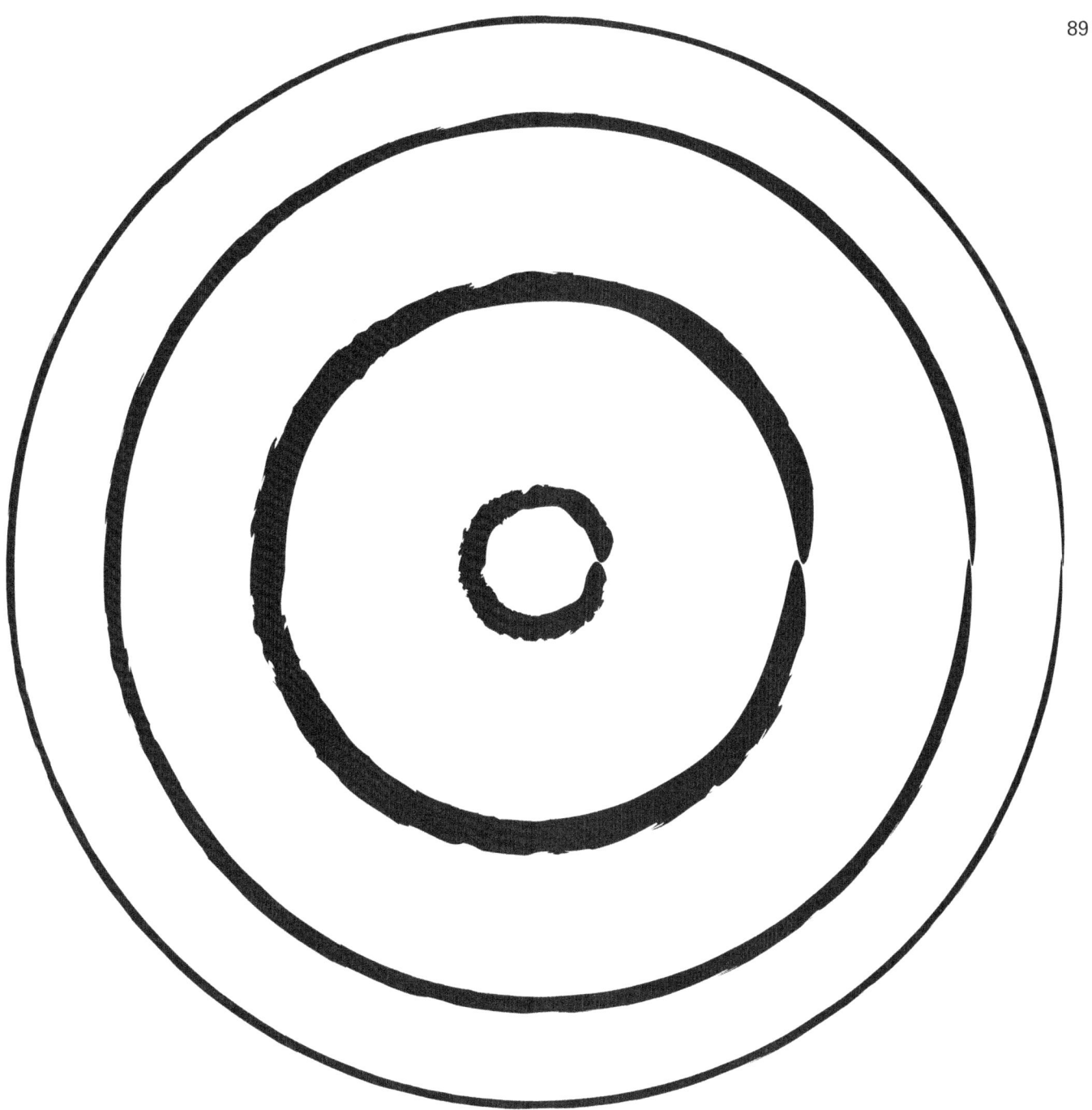

Now take a moment to celebrate the marvelous resource that is your community!

Our Natural State Is Calm

Practice relaxing, and regain your sense of calm.
Taking time and living purposefully are dreaming skills.

In February 2000 my son, Ben, his wife, Kristin, and I went to Africa on safari. We flew to Cairo, then to Nairobi, Kenya, and the next day took the five-hour bus ride across the border to Arusha, Tanzania. There we met our guide, Gabriel, and our driver, Mustafa, and began our tour.

I was excited to go on this trip, though I wasn't sure what to expect. Would we see the kind of dramatic animal scenes that are captured in films? What I didn't anticipate was the tremendous sense of calm I experienced in the game preserves, or how that sense of calm would influence me.

For our first look at the animals, Gabriel and Mustafa took us to the Ngorongoro Crater, an ancient volcanic caldera comprising a hundred square miles of grasslands, lakes, streams, and trees at the bottom of the deep, steep crater. The Ngorongoro Crater is home to twenty thousand large mammals and countless smaller animals and birds. We saw elephants and rare black rhinos, as well as dangerous hippos almost completely submerged in muddy water. We saw

warthogs and water buffalos, along with zebras resting their heads on the backs of other zebras. We saw wildebeests and elands, dik-diks and gazelles, baboons and monkeys. We saw pink flamingos, storks, and spoonbills. Tall, stilt-legged ostriches crossed our paths with their awkward run. We saw herons and ibis, bustards and coots. For all the activity, the atmosphere was peaceful.

Above the crater, we hiked into the surrounding Ngorongoro Conservation Area with a Maasai park ranger, Arkanini, on the lookout for animals. He carried a rifle just in case we met a dangerous one.

After a few days in the Ngorongoro, we drove to the vast expanse of the Serengeti Plain. In Tanzania alone, the Serengeti is the size of Connecticut, and the plain extends into southwest Kenya. The animals there are spread out—we drove from site to site to see them, directed at times by other tour drivers and guides, who slowed down to share information about animal sightings. On one such tip, we saw a herd of giraffes; on another, a leopard draped in the crotch of a tree; on another, a resting pride of lions.

The lions, about eight of them, were taking their ease in the shade of an acacia tree. Beside them, where the land rose gently, about two dozen zebras grazed peacefully. On the other side of the pride, a lone lioness, separate from the group, lounged in the shade of some bushes. As we watched, the zebras continued to munch, and the lions continued to rest. Everyone seemed relaxed and comfortable. After about ten minutes, the lioness got up, stretched, and began to walk—slink, really—slowly over toward the rest of the pride. As she did so, the zebra closest to the lions stopped grazing and raised its head to watch her, while all the other zebras continued to eat, seeming to take no notice of the lioness. She took her time settling down again, now under the acacia with her family. After she had been there for a few moments, the sentinel zebra went back to grazing, and the other zebras and the rest of the lions continued as before. All was well.

I commented to Gabriel about the peacefulness of the scene. The environment was calm, and I felt that calm. So much of what I had seen in films and elsewhere portrays the violence of the animals, their stampeding migrations, the chases, the kills. I hadn't expected this atmosphere of leisure and deep peacefulness. Gabriel said that's the way it usually is, though some tourists don't think they've gotten their money's worth unless they see a kill. Lions eat once every three days or so, and they hunt only when they're hungry. Otherwise they take it easy, and so do their prey.

On our second night in the Serengeti, we set up a camp in some trees on a small rise. After dinner, as we sat around the campfire, I began to feel nervous about sleeping alone in my tent. Gabriel assured me that in his twenty years of guiding and camping, none of his clients had experienced a dangerous incident. He added that he slept lightly, and if I felt afraid, I could call his name, and he would hear me. With that reassurance, I went into my tent and fell asleep.

I was awakened some time later by a series of breathy grunts and rustling sounds. *Uh oh*, I thought, and I felt a stab of fear. Then I saw the beam of Gabriel's flashlight and heard him moving about outside the tents. My tension grew as I continued to hear grunting and rustling and see the moving light. After a few minutes, the noises died away, the light went out, the night was dark and quiet again, and I gradually settled down and went back to sleep.

The next morning I said to Gabriel, "So, there was someone in our camp last night." "Yes," he said. "Who was it?" I asked. "A lioness," he answered. "Were we in danger?" I asked. "No," he said. A few years later my son told me that in fact a family of lions had strolled through our camp that night.

Soon after we had packed up camp and driven on, a lion walked across the road in front of our truck, a piece of meat from a fresh kill dangling from its mouth, and we heard the jackals braying as they waited nearby for their turn at the kill. We drove out of the Serengeti.

What I Learned: Our Natural State Is Calm

When I returned home from Africa, I reflected primarily on the pervasive sense of calm I experienced in the grasslands, and on my connection to the balance there. The animals in the wild live in an environment of calm punctuated by the anxiety of the hunt. My so-called civilized life resembles theirs. I also need food and protection from weather and the society of like beings. I also experience fight-or-flight responses when I perceive danger to myself and those close to me. And I, like the animals, enjoy a natural state of calm—for I now believe that calm is our natural state—when no danger is present.

That's the key: *when no danger is present*. At the time of the trip, my life was hectic. I worried about my work, which involved a great deal of travel, and

I struggled to balance work with family and play and time to do nothing. During that time, I was too often tense—alert for difficulties. I was manufacturing a constant sense of danger, as if I had to be poised at all times for fight or flight. And in that steady state of tension, I couldn't experience my natural calm.

When I returned from Africa, friends said I looked and sounded much calmer than I did before I left. I wanted to preserve the feelings I had had in the African grasslands. I started paying more attention to my emotions, noticing when I was tense, when my mind raced as if I were in danger, and I deliberately began to release that tension. I couldn't always manage it, but with practice I got better at it. I would notice the tension, ask myself if there was a good reason for it, find there wasn't, and do my belly breathing, stretch, and do whatever else I knew to do to let the tension go. As I stayed more relaxed, I noticed that my busy mind eased, my thinking lightened, I felt more generous toward other people and myself, and I was better able to maintain the grasslands calm.

What You Can Do

Our ability to create and maintain a sense of calm has a direct bearing on our ability to dream and to take steps to make our dreams come true. Creativity and imagination flourish when our minds are relaxed; when our pace is slower and we're not pushing ourselves or deliberately, insistently problem-solving; and certainly not when we're manufacturing a sense of danger, as I so often did.

Here is an example of how a couple responded to two instances of adversity, the second instance life-threatening, by making a series of creative decisions over the years that slowed them down and changed their lives. Their story illustrates many of the ideas in this book.

Richard and Joy met in the 1970s, when, as young teachers, they both applied for jobs at an inner-city high school undergoing a fresh start. In an attempt to give a failing school new life, a new administration came in, all existing faculty members had to reapply for their jobs, and teachers from other schools were encouraged to apply. Joy, already a faculty member at the school, was rehired and continued to teach English. Richard, a ceramicist teaching at another school, was hired to teach art. He was given an unfinished basement space in the building for use as his classroom and studio. In a departure from normal procedures, he and his students first renovated the space, taking most of a school year to do that. Then Richard began teaching drawing, painting, sculpture, and ceramics, making artists of his students against the odds. He and Joy flourished in their jobs, ultimately married, and, by the time they were approaching forty, had many years of teaching under their belts, no children, a carefree lifestyle, and little savings.

Trouble started when Richard was promoted to oversee art education in a small consortium of schools, including his own. He supervised art teachers at all grade levels but had no hiring or firing authority to go with his responsibility. He was discouraged by the chaotic nature of some of the classrooms and by how little some teachers were involved with their students. The satisfaction he experienced from the hands-on encouragement and development of his students eroded increasingly as more and more of his work became administrative and frustrating. Joy said, "He grew more tense and more critical until I hardly recognized the playful, creative man I had married." Richard said, "I hated the job."

Joy suggested that Richard quit and begin working on his own. She would be the one with the "proper job," as Richard called it, and he would become a working artist. Richard went for it. He leased a small studio and gallery, bought an ancient kiln and potter's wheel at auction with their small savings, and installed them in his new space. He learned to work around the quirks of his outdated equipment. He said, "I had to figure out what I could do with the old equipment. I tested the kiln for its highest heat and reduced from there, then found clay to fit the kiln." It took him a month to get up and running. Richard and Joy tightened their belts, and as Joy said, "Richard came back to himself and to me."

Over the next five years, Joy continued teaching, and Richard manufactured and sold his ceramics from the studio. Slowly he built his business. At the end of that time, their city took the studio property by right of eminent domain, and Richard lost his lease. In spite of that setback, and with the help of a small set-up grant, Richard and Joy rented another space closer to their home near the sea, and he moved the old equipment and his inventory. After a time, Joy was promoted to school principal, while Richard continued to work at the studio. Richard marketed his work himself, and a number of other galleries began to carry his ceramics. His business grew.

Joy, a perfectionist, worked hard to create a high school atmosphere both nurturing and demanding; she set high expectations for herself, her teachers, and the students. She worked as a principal in her intense and imaginative

way for ten years. Then one early morning in the middle of the school year, she collapsed, unable to get up to go to work. The collapse happened just one day after she had been diagnosed with very high blood pressure, so high that the doctor, new to her, advised her that her hypertension could be life-threatening and she should take time off immediately. Although Joy had no intention of not going to work, the collapse forced her to take sick leave and seek medical help. Ultimately her diagnosis was post-traumatic stress disorder, caused not by a single trauma or prolonged horror but by the accumulation of the day-in, day-out overload that characterized her approach to her work. After three months, still unable to work, Joy began to draw disability pay. After over a year of rest, medical care, and counseling, Joy and her doctors determined that she would not be able to return to her job.

In spite of this blow, Richard and Joy decided that he would continue to work independently, even as they realized that their reduced financial circumstances would continue. With the help of a financial planner and careful management, they were able to meet their bills. Richard closed his rented studio, added a small space to their modest home, and moved his workplace there. With rent savings, he bought a modern kiln and potter's wheel that enabled him to work more easily and in more varied ways. Managing her stress levels, Joy focused on gardening, working in her own yard and helping others with theirs. Richard and Joy, who had always enjoyed biking casually, began to bike more often and over longer distances, using their limited discretionary income for group bike trips around the country and, eventually, even abroad.

They are fourteen years into this new life. Now in his late sixties, Richard is nominally retired. He has scaled back his ceramics work and taken up sketching. When he and Joy travel, he no longer relies on a camera but has his sketchbook always at hand. They bike long distances for charity. Joy, not liking to ask for pledges, gardens for the neighbors who support their rides. Richard and Joy continue to budget carefully. Joy chooses her activities deliberately, excuses herself when she needs to pull back, and rests often. They live slowly, purposefully. They are noticeably relaxed, natural, easy, and interesting in conversation. They are appreciative of the opportunities they've had, though they would never have chosen the events that led to them. Joy says, "Our setbacks, absolutely including my illness, led us to a better life." Richard and Joy are happy with the choices they've made over the years, and, in their slowed-down way of living, they are thriving.

The story of Richard and Joy illustrates many overlapping and intertwining dreaming lessons. When Richard was unhappy with his work, they arranged for him to change it and tightened their belts accordingly. They knew that he, like all of us, deserved to love his work, to do the work he dreamed of doing. When Joy became ill and couldn't continue with her job, she and Richard did the necessary homework, got the help they needed, and made the required trade-offs for Richard to continue as a working artist and for Joy to get the rest that was essential for her health. They made each decision without knowing the longer-term outcomes, and they were ready to adjust when they had to. They trusted that they would have what they needed to manage, and they faced and dealt with every obstacle. They slowed down so that Joy could remain healthy and they could both enjoy their lives to the fullest.

When I met them, they were spending three months in Antigua as guests of an old friend, Graham, who had moved there, had space for them, and cherished their company. "Richard and Joy are lucky," you could say, and you would be right. And it was that long-term relationship with Graham that paved the way for this particular instance of luck. Richard and Joy show perfectly how our natural state is calm. Their serenity is contagious, and a short time in their presence reminded me again that staying relaxed is a key to making dreams come true.

Try This: Progressive Relaxation

Here is an exercise to help you with that most basic dreaming skill, one that Richard and Joy learned: relaxing. Any and all strategies for relaxing and staying relaxed are helpful. You probably already know what helps you, and if not, there are many books, tapes, videos, and online resources to help you. Here is one exercise that has helped me calm down at some of my most anxious times.

In this exercise, you'll tense and relax your muscles, one after another, and clearly feel the difference between a tense state and a relaxed one.

1. Get comfortable: no tight clothing, no shoes.
2. Do some belly breathing, and feel yourself relax.
3. Focus on your right foot. Tense the muscles in the foot, contracting them tightly. Hold for a slow count of ten.

4. Relax your foot. Pause, continuing to breathe for a slow count of ten.
5. Now focus on your left foot, and follow the same process: tense the muscles, pause for a count of ten, relax the muscles, and pause for a count of ten.
6. Go through the muscle groups listed below, contracting and releasing your muscles in the same way as you go. You can use the following order:

- right foot
- left foot
- right calf
- left calf
- right thigh
- left thigh
- hips and buttocks
- stomach
- chest
- back
- right arm and hand
- left arm and hand
- neck and shoulders
- face

If you have a way to make an audio recording, you can record directions for yourself, taking yourself through each muscle group progressively. Speak into the recorder calmly, or ask a friend whose voice you like to do so.

I have used progressive relaxation at night at times when I have been under stress and had trouble falling asleep. The exercise reminds me how differently tension and relaxation feel, and it helps me to stay relaxed.

Many other practices can help you achieve calm as well, including regular meditation, tai chi and other movement practices, and physical exercise. Whatever helps you gain and maintain calm will help you recognize and follow your dreams.

Now Consider This: Taking Time and Living Purposefully Are Dreaming Skills

In our natural, relaxed state, we can recognize more clearly that time is on our side: time to consider, time to decide, time to live intentionally. Taking time, being patient, and being mindful are not customary practices in our culture. And yet taking time is a prerequisite for living purposefully, and the two intertwined skills help us live as we wish to live, help us recognize and reach for our dreams.

My mother died in the summer of 2011, at age ninety-seven, and to the end she was purposeful about the way she lived. Eighteen years earlier, when my father died, Mom, though grieving, realized a long-held dream—one Dad did not share. At seventy-nine, she moved out of the house where we grew up and into an apartment in downtown Philadelphia. There was a park right across the street, and the world went by outside her door.

Mom continued to pursue her interests and enjoy herself, even as she aged and grew more frail. She used her free-flowing thinking to help herself continue to live as she wished, to make choices, unhurried, with the idea that time was on her side.

Mom valued family, friends, her synagogue, good food, classical music, art, theater, literature, the political process. She entertained family and friends for meals and tea; remembered with cards and gifts the birthdays of everyone in our extended family; worked as board secretary of her synagogue; attended the opera, and Philadelphia Orchestra concerts; belonged to the Philadelphia Museum of Art; took a poetry or fiction class each semester; continued to work, catering hors d'oeuvres and desserts for long-time customers; participated in her book club; attended lectures at the library; raised money for public radio; volunteered for political candidates and worked at the polls on elections days; walked every day; had her daily "four o'clock" (read: Scotch), sometimes with a neighbor; traveled domestically and internationally; looked her best; and kept an attractive, company-ready home.

Throughout her long life, Mom continued to be good company, and so she attracted good company. As she aged, it took her longer to do daily tasks, so she gave up some of her activities in order to be able to do others. She had

an instinctive understanding of what she wanted most, and she made her trade-offs. When she wasn't sure, she waited, set the question aside, and acted when the answer appeared.

She stopped catering at ninety, reluctantly, because she could no longer lift the pans. At ninety-two, she stopped fundraising for public radio. She also stopped taking two buses to the main library for the lecture series because lifting her walker onto the bus was daunting and she didn't like to ask the bus driver for help. Eventually, Mom stopped canvassing for her candidates, and when she was in her nineties and her passport came up for renewal, she let it expire. She no longer walked to the gym, doing exercises at home instead. After the 2008 elections, at ninety-four, she stopped working at the polls from six thirty AM to nine PM on election days because she thought she had become an imposition on the other poll workers. At ninety-five, two years before she died, she relinquished her job of taking minutes at synagogue board meetings.

Mom did, however, continue to go to lunch with friends on Tuesdays and to her writing class on Wednesdays. She continued to participate in her book club, attending her last meeting two weeks before she died. She entertained at home, though in her last few years she had an aide for a few hours each day who helped her shop, prepare food, do her exercises, and complete other tasks. She continued to have her four o'clock. She ordered clothing and gifts from catalogs to conserve her energy. In the spring of 2011 she attended the three events of her granddaughter's wedding, wearing new outfits for the rehearsal dinner on Friday and the wedding on Saturday night. For Sunday brunch, she wore a dress she already had. Mom put on her eye shadow before going out, and she wondered, a few weeks before she died, what would be the best way to whiten her teeth. She continued to go to the orchestra and theater. She visited us in Minneapolis each year, her last trip in the summer of 2010, when she was ninety-six.

Mom took the time she needed. During her last year, with the help of an interior decorator, she had the wall-to-wall carpeting in her living room taken up and replaced with an oriental rug. She told her children, apologetically, that she was spending our inheritance. "Go for it," we said. Even as her strength waned, Mom had time on her side.

As our society speeds up, we cram more into our days and become increasingly impatient for results. We press ourselves to make decisions quickly and expect others to do the same. We feel normal under pressure, we tout multitasking as a good thing, and some of us think a weekend off is a vacation.

All this hurry works against recognizing and realizing our dreams. Creative thinking springs from a relaxed mind. We may solve problems when we're pressed, since logical thinking can and does proceed from tension. But when we do this, we're drawing on memory and experience—what we already know—and not tapping into our creativity. We can repeat those processes we know, but we don't come up with anything new.

Imagination, creativity, and new ideas flower in slowed-down minds, and slowed-down minds require that most precious gift: time. If my mom in her nineties took the time she needed to discover what she really wanted, to make decisions and to make changes, can't we do that as well?

One Good Thing Leads to Another

When you least expect it, things come together.

By 2001, I had long dreamed of having a life partner, someone to whom I could make a lasting commitment. During the sixteen years since my divorce, I had dated some good men. But between my two seeming inabilities—one, to be a kind, generous, reliable, and interesting partner myself, and two, to attract, recognize, and appreciate someone with those characteristics—I had begun to doubt I'd ever make that dream come true. I could—and did—manage to fulfill many dreams, but for this one, I needed someone else's full cooperation. This dream was more complex.

One day in early January, I was on the phone with my aunt Sarah, who was eighty-five years old at the time. Aunt Sarah had always been romantic and was very fond of me. She lived in Florida, and I visited her once or twice a year when I traveled to work with my Florida clients. By the time of this telephone conversation, I had my small sailboat in a tiny marina on Lake Superior near the cabin. I was the only woman boat-owner there, and the guys in the

marina—all married—welcomed me to sail with them on their boats. I wanted to sail my own boat, yet was uncomfortable doing so alone in Lake Superior's unpredictable waters. When Aunt Sarah asked how my love life was, I replied that it was nonexistent. When I mentioned that I wished I could meet some single sailors, she gave me some advice.

"Why don't you put an ad in the personals column of the newspaper," she said, "as a way to meet sailors?" Or, more particularly in her mind, *a* sailor. She offered testimonials about children of friends who had found true love that way. And when I said, "Oh, no, Aunt Sarah, I'm not going to do that," she asked—no doubt with hand on hip and lips pursed—"And just what do you have to lose, Abby?" "Okay," I admitted, "I have nothing to lose." And I placed a short ad in the paper that very week that began, "Hey Sailor!"

Twenty-five middle-aged sailors answered the ad. One of them was Tom. He, like the others, left a message in the voice mailbox the newspaper supplied. His message—his voice, really—unlike the others, sent a shiver down my spine. When I called him, he invited me to his house for coffee, and I accepted. Later, I wondered what I'd been thinking, but I went there alone and didn't even take my dog, Cole.

That day, we talked and talked. He made dinner for me as we continued our conversation into the evening. Among many other things, I learned that Tom had a twenty-seven-foot sailboat in a Lake Superior marina not twenty miles from my marina, and for the last fifteen years of his teaching career, he had sailed his boat all summer, usually by himself, on the Great Lakes. And he had the same dream I had had for fifteen years: to live onboard a sailboat and travel.

Tom had just retired, and when I met him, he was about to leave for a three-month road trip. While he was gone, I enjoyed meeting other men who answered my ad, all the while looking forward to Tom's return. But during the time he was gone and the weeks that followed his planned date of return, I never heard from him.

Well, I had to do something. Tom didn't like the telephone, so, following my friend Jean's suggestion, I mailed Tom a note one day in early June, inviting him to lunch. The next day, Tom called to accept my invitation. After that lunch, we began to see each other regularly. We enjoyed the city's outdoor concerts, bike trails, and parks. We met each other's friends. We explored our Lake Superior haunts and sailed my little boat in the Apostle Islands. We agreed during that summer that if we were still together in the fall, we would start looking for a live-aboard sailboat online and, in January, begin boat shopping for real.

But Tom pulled back a number of times during the summer and fall of 2001, not sure that he really wanted a serious relationship. Each time he pulled back, I felt disappointed and upset. I relied on my African safari lessons to remind me of my natural state—calm. My upset feelings, I concluded, showed that my thinking was off, and I didn't want to have an important conversation with Tom when I was in that low mood. So I didn't protest, argue, or try to dissuade Tom. I simply said I was sorry to hear what he said, felt upset, and didn't agree, but if that's how he felt, he got to follow his own wishes. And I stepped back.

Each time, Tom abandoned his thoughts of leaving. Feeling no pressure from me whatsoever, he was back in the relationship right away. After the last pullback, just before we made our boat-shopping trip to the East Coast early in 2002, Tom stayed close.

And that's how I got my first dreamboat.

During our trip out east, Tom met my extended family in Philadelphia. We looked at boats in New England and made an offer on one, but the owner didn't accept it.

Online we found a similar boat for sale in Hyères, on the Mediterranean coast of France. By chance, we were planning a holiday to Paris in March, so we decided to take the high-speed train from there to see the yacht. We liked what we saw and considered making an offer. Then the French broker told us about another boat he knew of, newly on the market: a thirty-seven-foot Sweden Yachts sloop. The boat was in a marina two hours down the coast of the Riviera, between Nice and Monaco. Would we be willing to drive down with him to take a look? Tough duty, but we gritted our teeth and headed south.

As soon as we went aboard, we knew we had found our boat. Our sea trial confirmed our choice. She was a four-year-old fiberglass yacht, newer than anything we had looked at, a strongly built performance cruiser that would sail close to the wind and be responsive to sail set. She was beautifully finished inside and out, with a white hull (coolest in the Mediterranean heat) and teak decks that were handsome and solid underfoot. Her interior cabins were well designed, outfitted with creature comforts and modern technical instruments, and finished in glowing mahogany. Her sails were like new, and her cockpit was

comfortable, with bench seats long enough to pass my nap test. In all, she was more than we could have wished for: newer, faster, more strongly built, more beautiful. The dollar was strong against the euro then, bringing the asking price within range, and the owner accepted our offer.

In mid-April we returned to France to close on the boat. Then we flew back to the United States, and, between April 15 and July 2, we managed with the help of friends to sell two houses, two cars, one small boat, and one piano. We sold or gave away most of our other possessions, storing the rest in friends' basements. I closed my business. We got married on June 30 and settled Cole, now ten years old, with my brother and his family. (We couldn't take Cole with us—for me the only difficult aspect of our decision to go sailing.) On July 2, we again flew to France, this time to take up residence on our boat, renamed *Bloom*, our first home together.

We had done far too much in so short a time. Perhaps we should have been more sensible and taken more time to plan. But at fifty-eight and sixty-three we enjoyed our first year of marriage on board our new boat in the south of France. We kept the original owner's slip in the seaside town of St. Jean Cap Ferrat, and the marina there became our base. We took *Bloom* out for early cruises, called "shakedown cruises," to get to know her. We sailed to nearby ports in France—Villefranche, Antibes, Menton—and to San Remo, in Italy. In the fall, we took our first overnight cruise to the French island of Corsica, ninety miles away. We spent six weeks there before returning to mainland France.

That fall and winter, we took the bus to Nice and explored its neighborhoods and attractions. We visited the small towns near our harbor and found our favorite markets and cafés. On calm days, we motored in our dinghy to a large supermarket in Monaco where we did our major grocery shopping. The following spring, 2003, we left our slip at Cap Ferrat and headed east to Corsica again, then into Italian waters and through Ionian and Aegean Greece, reaching the south coast of Turkey in the fall, seven months after we left France.

After two glorious sailing seasons in Turkey, we headed back west across the Mediterranean, visiting new ports and revisiting favorite ones. We spent time in Spain—in the Balearic Islands and on mainland Spain as well.

In 2006, we sailed to Gibraltar. I remember on the calm evening of that twenty-six-hour trip, dolphins escorted us, diving and swimming on both sides of our bow. Tom and I went up to the foredeck to watch them, and called hello to two on the starboard side. They looked right up, and dolphins and humans smiled at each other. Leaving the Mediterranean Sea, we sailed through the Strait of Gibraltar, explored the Atlantic coasts of Spain and Portugal, and then headed south to the Canary Islands in the fall. In December, we crossed the Atlantic Ocean, a three-week trip, sailing west with the trade winds to Trinidad and the islands of the Caribbean. We've been spending our winters cruising the Caribbean ever since.

Tom had known from the start that he wanted to cross the Atlantic, but I was fearful of such a trip. I was always a bit nervous when we set sail because, even with good weather reporting, conditions at sea are unpredictable. But we prepared well for our trips; we had a strong boat and skills to match; and once we set sail, I relaxed. Still, the prospect of the long trip on the open sea to the Western Hemisphere was daunting.

On the way from southern Portugal to the Canary Islands, several events happened in close succession that finally dispelled my fear of crossing. The first event was scary. During the beginning of that six-day trip the weather was rough, with thirty-knot winds where fifteen knots had been predicted. The wind and waves were from the northeast, but a sea swell came at us from the northwest, driven by a hurricane-strength storm off the United Kingdom. This resulted in a confused sea, and the boat movement was very uncomfortable. Also, on our first day, a rogue wave, which looked as tall as our fifty-two-foot mast, suddenly loomed behind us. It lifted us, *Bloom* rising higher and higher, until the top of the wave broke over her stern. The wave drenched us, filled the cockpit, and then quickly drained out through the scuppers in the cockpit floor. We were fine, but that experience didn't encourage my confidence about crossing the Atlantic, at least not at first. I told Tom that I wanted nothing to do with another long passage. I was done.

After three days, the weather settled, and for the rest of the trip conditions were perfect: calm seas, fifteen knots of wind from behind us, cloudless blue skies. Heaven. Then, on our last night at sea, while I was on watch and Tom slept, I saw a large flaming bright green ball, with a tail trailing behind it, arc through the sky. I watched, transfixed, as it descended and, after a few moments, disappeared. Tom thought the flaming ball must have been a meteorite—and he wished he had seen it, too. The next morning, with the Canary

Islands in sight, we were joined by a school of dolphins for a while. Somehow, as we sailed into the Canaries, my fear of crossing the ocean disappeared. I don't know why exactly, but it seemed that *Bloom*'s sturdy handling of the rogue wave, my awe at the fiery green ball in the sky, the smooth sailing, and playful dolphins at the end of our trip combined to inspire and reassure me. The natural world was on my side, and I was ready to cross the Atlantic.

That fall Tom and I relaxed at anchor in the Canary Islands, until the trade winds began to blow. Then, in early December, we left our mooring and set our sails for the downwind run west, and those reliable winds blew us all the way to Trinidad.

As Tom and I look back now on our sailing adventures in the Mediterranean, crossing the Atlantic, and in the Caribbean, we marvel that our life together on board and at sea, the friends we've made, and the places we've seen have exceeded our dreams.

What I Learned: When You Least Expect It, Things Come Together

Everything I learned from pursuing my other dreams came together as I pursued and realized these two big ones. In the first instance, seeking my dream guy, I let Aunt Sarah nudge me into doing something new, and I placed the ad. I traded comfort for the nervousness that comes with meeting potentially datable strangers. As it happened, I was able to relax and enjoy my conversations with quite a few interesting men. After Tom and I got together, I let him go when he got cold feet, as difficult as that was, clarifying my strong preferences and respecting his.

In the second instance, both Tom and I made the trade-offs necessary to finance the yacht and our life aboard, selling our homes and getting rid of most of our possessions. We kept art, books, music, and a few antiques. We set sail with no real estate to fall back on except the cabin, though we eventually bought a small condo, now our home when we're in Minneapolis. For us, the chance to experience our dream adventure outweighed the pleasures and security of owning a house filled with things.

Although many of us associate risk with taking action, inaction also carries risks: those of missed opportunity and regret. If Tom and I hadn't tried to live our dream life, we would have wondered forever, *What if . . . ?* and *Why didn't we . . . ?* For us, not going for the dream seemed riskier than reaching for it.

If our sailing dream had not worked out, we could have made other decisions, found another house, settled into a different life. As it turned out, our sailing life has suited us perfectly and is the culmination of all previous dreams.

What You Can Do

Not everyone experiences successive smaller dreams converging into a large one, as I did. But one dream may well lead to another simply because of our practice: we get used to thinking in terms of what we would really like, to noticing opportunities and pursuing them. The process becomes an integral part of our lives—it becomes habitual.

As we enjoy our successes and reflect back on them, we become more confident and more intimately familiar with what we like doing and what we do well.

Here's an exercise to help you review your successes.

Try This: Glory Days

The purpose of this exercise is to help you review some of your successes, with an eye toward including elements of those successes in future adventures.

First, list three to five things you have accomplished. These achievements don't have to involve anybody else's applause or qualify as worldly success. For example, when I first did this exercise, my list included giving a dinner party, stripping wallpaper and painting a room, earning a teaching certificate, learning a new language, and taking the whitewater canoe clinic. Your achievements, too, may be big or small. They should be accomplishments that you are proud of, that make you feel happy, competent, confident.

LIST OF ACHIEVEMENTS:

1. _____

2. _____

3. _____

4. _____

5. _____

Second, describe each achievement in the spaces provided below. Include details like how you decided to do this, how you began, the process you followed—what happened along the way—and the results. Then answer the following four questions:

1. What did you learn from this experience? What, if anything, surprised you? How did you feel as you went through and finished the experience? (Don't apologize, disclaim, or second-guess!)
2. What about the experience did you enjoy? Name three to five elements, or threads, that you would like to repeat or preserve with other experiences.
3. What was not enjoyable or not desirable? What were the elements you would rather avoid in the future?
4. What else might you do to incorporate the enjoyable and satisfying elements of this accomplishment into your life?

ACHIEVEMENT #1:

_____

Describe this achievement—how you began, the process you followed, and the results:

_____
_____
_____
_____
_____
_____
_____
_____
_____

1. What did you learn from this experience? What, if anything, surprised you? How did you feel as you went through and finished the experience? (Don't apologize, disclaim, or second-guess!)

_____
_____
_____
_____
_____
_____

2. What about the experience did you enjoy? Name three to five elements, or threads, that you would like to repeat or preserve with other experiences.

_____
_____
_____
_____
_____
_____
_____

3. What was not enjoyable, not desirable? What were the elements you would rather avoid in the future?

_____
_____
_____
_____
_____

4. What else might you do to incorporate the enjoyable and satisfying elements of this accomplishment into your life?

_____
_____
_____
_____
_____

ACHIEVEMENT #2:

_____

Describe this achievement—how you began, the process you followed, and the results:

_____
_____
_____
_____
_____
_____
_____
_____
_____
_____

1. What did you learn from this experience? What, if anything, surprised you? How did you feel as you went through and finished the experience? (Don't apologize, disclaim, or second-guess!)

_____
_____
_____
_____

2. What about the experience did you enjoy? Name three to five elements, or threads, that you would like to repeat or preserve with other experiences.

_____
_____
_____
_____
_____
_____
_____

3. What was not enjoyable, not desirable? What were the elements you would rather avoid in the future?

_____
_____
_____
_____
_____

4. What else might you do to incorporate the enjoyable and satisfying elements of this accomplishment into your life?

_____
_____
_____
_____
_____

ACHIEVEMENT #3:

_____

Describe this achievement—how you began, the process you followed, and the results:

_____
_____
_____
_____
_____
_____
_____
_____
_____

1. What did you learn from this experience? What, if anything, surprised you? How did you feel as you went through and finished the experience? (Don't apologize, disclaim, or second-guess!)

_____
_____
_____
_____
_____

2. What about the experience did you enjoy? Name three to five elements, or threads, that you would like to repeat or preserve with other experiences.

_____
_____
_____
_____
_____
_____
_____

3. What was not enjoyable, not desirable? What were the elements you would rather avoid in the future?

_____
_____
_____
_____
_____

4. What else might you do to incorporate the enjoyable and satisfying elements of this accomplishment into your life?

_____
_____
_____
_____
_____

ACHIEVEMENT #4: _____

Describe this achievement—how you began, the process you followed, and the results:

_____
_____
_____
_____
_____
_____
_____
_____
_____
_____

1. What did you learn from this experience? What, if anything, surprised you? How did you feel as you went through and finished the experience? (Don't apologize, disclaim, or second-guess!)

_____
_____
_____
_____

2. What about the experience did you enjoy? Name three to five elements, or threads, that you would like to repeat or preserve with other experiences.

_____
_____
_____
_____
_____
_____
_____

3. What was not enjoyable, not desirable? What were the elements you would rather avoid in the future?

_____
_____
_____
_____
_____

4. What else might you do to incorporate the enjoyable and satisfying elements of this accomplishment into your life?

_____
_____
_____
_____
_____

ACHIEVEMENT #5:

Describe this achievement—how you began, the process you followed, and the results:

1. What did you learn from this experience? What, if anything, surprised you? How did you feel as you went through and finished the experience? (Don't apologize, disclaim, or second-guess!)

2. What about the experience did you enjoy? Name three to five elements, or threads, that you would like to repeat or preserve with other experiences.

   _____
   _____
   _____
   _____
   _____

3. What was not enjoyable, not desirable? What were the elements you would rather avoid in the future?

   _____
   _____
   _____
   _____
   _____

4. What else might you do to incorporate the enjoyable and satisfying elements of this accomplishment into your life?

   _____
   _____
   _____
   _____
   _____

Now use the space below to reflect on any realizations, insights, and aha moments you have gained as a result of doing this exercise, and how you might apply this learning from past experiences to future adventures.

Closing Words: Take Charge of Your Life

Now you might be thinking about the reasons why I—and others—can make dreams come true but you can't. You might be thinking: *Oh, but she's bolder than I am.* Or, *She's so experienced.* Or, *Oh, she can travel.* Or, *She's written a book. So of course she can conjure up a dream and make it come true.*

Why look for reasons you *can't* do something you'd like to do or ways in which you're different from those folks who go ahead with their dreams? Why not look for reasons you *can* do something, ways you're similar to those lucky folks who, right now, are doing what they love?

The difference between those who do and those who don't is that some folks proceed. They realize what they want, they plan, they make compromises and trade-offs, they decide some dreams aren't worth the cost, they take their time, and they rely on their community for support. And although they may not realize their dreams right away, they take charge of their lives. You can do that too.

Don't let habitual negative thinking get in your way. Begin small if you have to, but begin. Be willing to start down the path without knowing where it will end. Give yourself plenty of breathing room. Notice what you love. Let your ideas and insights come. They will, and you'll be glad.

Once you've started, please tell me how you're doing. I'd love to know how any part of this book has encouraged you to pursue your most cherished dreams. Please contact me at dreaminglessons@gmail.com. I look forward to hearing from you. Good luck!

Additional Notes

ADDITIONAL NOTES

ADDITIONAL NOTES

CPSIA information can be obtained at www.ICGtesting.com
Printed in the USA
LVOW03s2226250815

451559LV00011B/152/P

9 780986 431807